Professional Behaviors in Athletic Training

Professional Behaviors in Athletic Training

Susan E. Hannam, HSD, ATC, CHES
Slippery Rock University
Slippery Rock, PA

SLACK
INCORPORATED

6900 Grove Rd. • Thorofare, NJ 08086

The work SLACK Incorporated publishes is peer reviewed. Prior to publication, recognized leaders in the field, educators, and clinicians provide important feedback on the concepts and content that we publish. We welcome feedback on this work.

Hannam, Susan Elizabeth.
     Professional Behaviors in Athletic Training/Susan Hannam.
        p. cm.
     Includes bibliographical references and index.
     ISBN 1-55642-409-4 (alk. paper)
     1. Athletic Trainers. I. Title.

     RC1210.H28 2000
     617.1'027--dc21   00--30068

Printed in the United States of America.
Published by: SLACK Incorporated
                  6900 Grove Road
                  Thorofare, NJ 08086 USA
                  Telephone: 856-848-1000
                  Fax: 856-853-5991
                  www.slackbooks.com

Contact SLACK Incorporated for more information about other books in this field or about the availability of our books from distributors outside the United States.

Last digit is print number: 10 9 8 7 6 5 4 3 2

DEDICATION

This book is dedicated to my former students, who over the years have taught me humility in the awareness that they do what I do—not what I say—and have filled me with awe at their tremendous capacity to learn and develop.

CONTENTS

ACKNOWLEDGMENTS

To my mentors:

Ms. Marje Albohm, whose influence greatly affected my professional development and who continues to blaze trails for others while consistently role modeling and demonstrating a genuine passion for the profession;

Dr. S. Kay Burrus, who exudes professionalism and whose absence during the writing of this book (owing to illness) caused me to reflect deeply to try to capture her essence and approval of all that was written;

Dr. John Schrader, who has always provided encouragement, had faith in me, and been supportive of my efforts; and

Sr. Rose Ann Trzil, who has served as a role model and continues to teach me how to follow my path with authenticity, integrity, dignity, humility, and gratitude.

To others:

Drs. Mary Adair, Anne Griffiths, Martha Haversitick, Sharon Johnson, James Laux, Catherine Morsink, Leona Parascenzo, and Pat Zimmerman, who provided wisdom and suggestions for development of the book;

Ms. Sharon Isacco and Patti Pink for assistance and support in typing the manuscript; and

My teachers, former classmates, and colleagues in the field who continue to remind me, through their words and deeds, of the many behaviors that epitomize true professionalism.

The Slippery Rock University athletic training classes of 2000 and 2001 and faculty members Bonnie Siple and Todd Evans who allowed their work to be photographed for the book.

ABOUT THE AUTHOR

Susan E. Hannam, HSD, ATC, CHES, is a full professor in the Allied Health Department and Assistant to the Dean of the College of Health and Human Services at Slippery Rock University, Slippery Rock, PA. This is Dr. Hannam's 13th year at Slippery Rock University, where she served as a faculty member and head football athletic trainer for 4 years and later became a curriculum program director. She also serves as Co-Coordinator of Continuous Improvement for the university.

Dr. Hannam has more than 20 years of teaching experience and has served on the faculty of athletic training curriculum programs at Acadia University, Wolfville, Nova Scotia, Western Illinois University, Macomb, IL, and Indiana University, Bloomington, IN. She has 16 years of clinical experience, serving as head athletic trainer at Acadia University and head women's athletic trainer at Western Illinois University and Indiana University.

Dr. Hannam was a member of the National Athletic Trainers' Association (NATA) Education Task Force and chaired the subcommittee on undergraduate education. She was also involved with planning the first NATA Research Education Foundation Educators' Conference. She has authored several journal articles and presented at numerous national and international conferences on assessment and learning and substance abuse. Currently she is involved with research on critical thinking skills and dispositions among undergraduate athletic training students, as well as learning styles and their relationship to success in distance education.

She was graduated from Acadia University with a Bachelor of Science in Physical Education and from Indiana University with a Master of Science in Athletic Training and a Doctorate in Health and Safety. She is a licensed public school teacher, a certified athletic trainer, a certified health education specialist, and Myers–Briggs Type Indicator assessment qualified.

PREFACE

Recent major and far-reaching changes in health care continue to create challenges and opportunities for the health-related professions and health care practitioners. Dramatic and revolutionary shifts in health care funding and delivery and advances in technology are high on the list of factors that are precipitating major educational reform and changing job markets and where and how we work. Competition for scarce resources grows daily. The National Athletic Trainers' Association (NATA) has responded to these challenges with its increased emphasis on education programs via the Education Council, its expanded research opportunities through the Research and Education Foundation, and a membership that is increasing in number and diversity (the number of certified athletic trainers more than doubled between 1990 and 1999). Curriculum programs are preparing students to graduate with knowledge, skills, and abilities that reflect the current and future needs of the profession and the physically active. Students must demonstrate mastery of the cognitive, psychomotor, and affective domains of the *Athletic Training Educational Competencies*[1] and complete clinical requirements before being permitted to take the NATA Board of Certification (NATABOC) examination. These competencies are woven into rigorous curriculum courses and clinical experiences. As a result of their educational process, prior experiences, and a host of other variables, students also develop behaviors that influence how they and ultimately the profession are perceived by other professions and society at large. These behaviors often become automatic and routine, almost at a subconscious level, yet they have the potential to effect significant positive or disastrous consequences on the profession.

This book is written with the intent of identifying for students some of those everyday situations where one has the choice to either respond as a true professional or be unaware of what is happening and react in ways that might not portray the most desirable image. Many of these skills and abilities are difficult to define, and even harder to measure, but are just as important as cognitive and clinical skills in terms of success in getting and keeping a job and maintaining the image of our profession.

Many of the affective competencies in the Professional Development and Responsibilities and Health Care Administration domains of the *Athletic Training Educational Competencies*[1] are germane to the content of this book. These have been identified at the beginning of appropriate chapters.

Chapters 1 through 3 trace the evolution of the health professions and identify the hallmarks of true health care professionals. There has been an ongoing debate about the definition of a professional, and insight is provided to help understand why we, as athletic trainers, deserve equal standing with other professionals. In addition, at the heart of all professions is a code of ethics. Comparisons are made between the NATA code and other select health care professions' codes. The professional responsibilities of members of the NATA and implications of the rapidly changing workplace are also discussed.

Chapters 4 through 7 address many of the professional skills (not necessarily taught in any formal way) of which one must be aware if one is to continue to build an image as a health care professional. Networking, communication and interpersonal skills, recognition of cultural differences, manners, civility, and attitudes are some of the areas explored.

Chapters 8 through 10 discuss professional ways to prepare oneself for job searching, the importance of teamwork in today's workplace, getting established in a new workplace, and the importance and necessity of lifelong learning.

Writing this book has been an enjoyable, yet challenging, task. As a teacher and clinical instructor of many athletic training students over the last 20 years, I have always been aware of the fact that students, athletes, and others are observing my actions and that those actions speak much more loudly than anything I say. The enormity of the responsibility to role model in ways that respect the integrity of the position (in various roles including as a certified athletic trainer and curriculum director) and to promote the athletic training profession in positive ways is not to be taken lightly. Today, more than ever before, we all must do our part to insure that this profession remains respected by other health care professionals and the public. This book has provided me with an opportunity to reflect on and refine the concepts that I have had the privilege of being taught or role modeled over the years by some of the finest professionals in the field. It is my hope that in some small way, the pages will speak to the reader and make a difference.

REFERENCE

1. National Athletic Trainers' Association. *Athletic Training Educational Competencies.* Dallas, TX: National Athletic Trainers' Association; 1999.

Chapter One

Professions, Professionals, and Professionalism

"If you wish to converse with me, define your terms."
Voltaire

OBJECTIVES

On completion of this chapter, the student will be able to accomplish the following:

- Explain the reasons for debate over the definition of a profession
- Describe the components necessary to ensure professionalism
- Explain the attributes of a professional
- Discuss the future challenges facing the athletic training profession

PROFESSIONS

Whereas most people have a general idea of what is meant by the word "profession," there is a surprising amount of debate over the word's meaning. This debate goes back to the early 1900s and is found mainly in the social sciences literature. Health and medical fields have only recently joined in the discussion, primarily owing to how the changing health care and business worlds now affect the various health care professions.

Because the past work was done by a variety of academic disciplines, it should come as no surprise that there is no consensus in the literature on the definition of the word profession. Some believe that a precise definition is possible; others believe the term is used so widely that it would be impossible to define. Some even suggest that the term professional be eliminated.[1]

An understanding of the history of all professions, as well as knowledge of the current issues facing health care professions in particular, creates a foundation from which to advocate the athletic training profession. To that end, the *Athletic Training Educational Competencies*[2] require that students be proficient in competencies related to professional development. This text primarily deals with the affective domains (see Appendix A). Discussion in this chapter is relevant to the following competencies under the domain of Professional Development & Responsibility:

- Advocates the National Athletic Trainers' Association (NATA) as an allied health professional organization dedicated to the care of athletes and others involved in physical activity
- Respects the role and responsibilities of other health care professions
- Defends the responsibility to interpret and promote athletic training as a professional discipline among allied health professional groups and the general public

A BRIEF HISTORY

Debate over the definition of a profession has existed since the early 20th century. The issues include which occupations should be called professions and what criteria should constitute a profession. There is further controversy about when professions may have first emerged, and again the debate centers around how one defines a profession.

Alfred Whitehead (cited in Cogan[3]) believed that the root of professions could be found in the teaching and followers of Plato, Aristotle, and the Stoics. Others say there is no evidence of the hallmarks of a profession during these early times and that a Greek lawyer was merely a friend of the litigant rather than a specialist. Similarly, they argue, in ancient times physicians were merely students of nonprofessional practitioners. The Roman physician was usually a slave. Authors such as Carr-Saunders[4] and Wilson[4], writing in the 1920s, believed that accountants, architects, and engineers were customarily salaried administrators employed by the state. They had no organized training schools nor did they constitute a distinct social group.

Regardless of the thoughts about the origin of early professions, the true antecedents of professions were found in 11th century Europe.[4] Surgeons, teachers, clergy, and lawyers organized into associations, and soon universities formed to train these specialists. In 1928, Carr-Saunders stated that "Every profession in its early days has to fight for a proper recognition."[4] This helped lead to the development of professional associations. In the late 1800s, the National Union of Teachers formed, with its stated objective "To raise the status of the teaching profession."

When professions emerge, members attempt to form professional associations to serve their common interests. This may take some time. In the athletic training profession, for instance, we know that there were practicing athletic trainers in ancient Greece. Dr. S.E. Bilik is identified as the father of modern athletic training, working as a student athletic trainer, athletic trainer, and team physician at the University of Illinois in Chicago in 1914.[5] The modern movement began with men meeting at competition sites as they cared for athletic teams. The yearning to share ideas grew, and the first national meeting of athletic trainers was held in 1938 at the Drake Relays in Des Moines, Iowa.[5] The current NATA was formed in 1950 with its first meeting in Kansas City, Missouri. Women were permitted to join the profession in the early 1970s, with the first woman certified in 1973.[5]

DEFINITIONS

According to Carr-Saunders, "A profession may perhaps be defined as an occupation based upon specialized intellectual study and training, the purpose of which is to supply skilled service or advice to others for a definite fee or salary."[4] However, more current definitions of a profession vary. The *Oxford English Dictionary*[6] states:

the occupation which one professes to be skilled in and to follow:
(a) A vocation in which a professed knowledge of some department of learning or science is used in its application to the affairs of others or in the practice of an art founded upon it
(b) In a wider sense: any calling or occupation by which a person habitually earns his living

Webster's New Word Dictionary of American English[7] defines profession as:

1. A professing, or declaring; avowal
2. A vocation, or occupation requiring advanced education and training, and involving intellectual skills, as medicine, law, theology, engineering, teaching, etc.

The United States Department of Labor defines a profession as an occupation and recognizes over 1200 of them. Athletic trainer is listed under specialty occupations. The etymology of our term "professional" can be traced to *profiteri*—to acknowledge; to confess; to profess, avow before all, publicly.[8]

CURRENT DEBATE

The definition debate has continued in the social sciences and is becoming more widely publicized in the health care field because of the changes and implications in health care reform. Services provided by physicians, for example, are now often seen as being provided for financial gain rather than for a minimal fee. Purists would say that this no longer meets the criteria of a profession.

Cruess and Cruess list 9 characteristics of professions (Table 1-1).[1] They contend that at the heart of every profession is legally sanctioned control over a specialized body of knowledge and a commitment of services. This framework of characteristics will be used as the modern definition of profession for this text. In addition, many authors refer to a professional's *fiduciary role*—worthy of trust whether under contract or not.[5,10]

PROFESSIONALS

Distinguishing between amateur and professional status cannot be the only criterion to define a professional. For instance, in some disciplines, someone who simply takes a fee for performing a service that others (amateurs) do for free is called a professional. There is nothing especially honorable in this sense of being a nonamateur.[10] Without considering professionalism's criteria and definitions, however, many groups have latched onto the term professional to help their image.

Table 1-1

A PROFESSION POSSESSES A DISCRETE BODY OF KNOWLEDGE AND SKILLS OVER WHICH ITS MEMBERS HAVE EXCLUSIVE CONTROL

1. The work based upon this knowledge is controlled and organized by associations that are independent of both the state and capital.

2. The mandate of these associations is formalized by a variety of written documents, which include laws covering licensure and regulations granting authority.

3. Professional organizations serve as the ultimate authorities on the personal, social, economic, cultural, and political affairs relating to their domains. They are expected to influence public policy and inform the public within their areas of expertise.

4. Admission to professions requires a long period of education, and the professions are responsible for determining the qualifications and (usually) the numbers of those to be educated for practice, the substance of their training, and the requirements for its completion.

5. Within the constraints of the law, the professions control admission to practice and the terms, conditions, and goals of the practice itself.

6. The professions are responsible for the ethical and technical criteria by which their members are evaluated and have the exclusive right to discipline unprofessional conduct.

7. Individual members remain autonomous in their workplaces within the limits of rules and standards laid down by their associations and the legal structures within which they work.

8. It is expected that professionals will gain their livelihoods by providing service to the public in the area of their expertise.

9. Members are expected to value performance above reward and are held to higher standards of behavior than are nonprofessionals.

Adapted from Cruess and Cruess.[1]

For example, in the yellow pages of telephone books, one can find "professional" karate centers, pest control companies, and temporary workers. It is not uncommon to pass vehicles on the highway with labels proclaiming "Professional Painters," "Professional Cleaning Service," "Professional Landscapers"—the examples go on and on. Certainly workers want recognition and honor and any status (name) that might give them credibility and more pay. This does not justify the use of the term profession in its pure sense.

State licensing is also not sufficient in determining professional status—many states license barbers, beauticians, and others who call themselves "professionals" in the nonamateur sense. Moline states:

> "We assume that the professional knows what is good for us, but that is not enough. It is possible to know what is good for a person and not care to facilitate this. Our ideal of the professional assumes not just a willingness to facilitate what is good for us, but a very strong lifetime commitment to facilitating it. It assumes that the person who approaches this ideal of the professional has come to have his or her entire life revolve around service to patients, clients, or members of the congregation. It assumes that this service is the person's top priority or very nearly so, ranking above the professional's own convenience, comfort, or financial security. It assumes that the professional's identity lies in service to the overall good of the client, not simply in doing a job for the client."[10]

Moline also suggests that we contrast people who have a job, occupation, or trade with those who have a calling. He believes that having a calling is a hallmark of professionals. The athletic training profession certainly meets this standard. In fact, the athletic trainer puts the athlete and the team ahead of him- or herself and often is in a position where commitment to the welfare of the team takes priority over even his or her personal life and family. Athletic trainers often speak about what "I am" versus what "I do for a living." Moline would categorize this identity as a calling.

PROFESSIONALISM

This chapter has demonstrated that vigorous criteria must be met in order to be recognized and honored as a profession. The athletic training profession meets these criteria. This section will focus on the practical extension of being a professional—professionalism. *The Random House Dictionary of the English Language*[11] defines "professionalism" as:

1. Professional character, spirit, or methods
2. The standing, practice, or methods of a professional, as distinguished from an amateur.

All professions are under constant external and internal scrutiny when it comes to professionalism. It is one of the most necessary yet least focused upon skills that can be learned as one develops first as a student, then through entry level in the profession, and finally into a mature, contributing professional. This development is so important that the rest of this book is dedicated to giving practical insight and advice on how handling daily events and situations can make significant differences in one's personal growth and the growth of athletic training. Professionalism must be taught. Students (and the profession) cannot afford to ignore this critical aspect of professional development.

At the heart of professionalism is the upholding of the organization's code of ethics. NATA's code of ethics clearly sets the standard of behavior expected of each and every certified athletic trainer. Jordan Cohen suggests that "the phenomenal changes taking place in our health care system make it essential for us to know, at the most fundamental level, who we are and what we do."[12] Codes of ethics preserve the integrity of the profession, prevent misrepresentation among professionals, and protect the public from fraud and unethical behavior.[13] Failure to maintain this standard can result in losing membership in the association and losing certification. Codes of ethics will be discussed in more detail in Chapter 2.

Freidson[8] believes that maintaining professional status will require a major effort to teach professionals their obligations. The following components (modified from Cruess and Cruess[1]) are suggested as necessary in order to ensure that professionalism is learned by students in the field of athletic training:

1. The concept that to be a professional is not a right but a privilege with a long history and tradition of healing and service must be emphasized.
2. Identifiable educational content in the undergraduate curriculum must be devoted to professionalism, and this should be reinforced in postgraduate programs and in continuing education. Knowledge of the subject should be part of the evaluation of all students.
3. Professionalism must be clearly defined and its characteristics identified.

4. Professionalism should be identified as an ideal to be constantly pursued, stressing its inherent moral value. The concept of altruism and "calling" must be emphasized as essential to professionalism.
5. A knowledge of general codes of ethics governing the conduct of the professional as well as the philosophical and historical derivations of these codes should be covered.
6. The nature of the collective autonomy of the profession, along with its legitimate and inherent limitations, should be outlined.
7. Teaching should include relevant material drawn from sociology, philosophy, economics, political science, and medical ethics as related to professionalism and specifically should contain interpretations of both the course of events and athletic trainer behaviors that are critical in the profession. The profession must not be allowed to build and maintain its own myths while avoiding ideas that challenge them.
8. The link between professional status and obligations to society that must be fulfilled to maintain public trust must be recognized.

FUTURE CHALLENGES

Professions are being challenged by many external forces such as the changing health care system, informed and demanding clients, government mandates, and competition. It is a time for all professionals to be aware of the issues facing their professions and to be actively involved in dialogue about these issues with colleagues.

To continue to be effective and remain viable, professions may need to drop some of their boundaries and begin to share information and skills. The number one question that professions must consider, to meet the criteria for a profession, is: "How can the patient/client receive the best possible care?" This question needs to be answered without regard to legal and administrative changes or internal or external criticisms. This question is far more important than "How can we make our profession dominant?"—a quality that does not meet the criteria for a profession, although this goal appears to be the current focus of many health professions. If the number one purpose is to meet the needs of the patient/client, the professional also must examine ways to work with other professions to ensure that all of the patient's needs are addressed.

The health professions are unsure about how the many changes in the health care system (eg, third party reimbursement, managed care) will affect them. Some argue that health reforms threaten professionalism.[14] Certainly professions will continue to be necessary, as well as increasingly scrutinized, entities. In the past, the norm has been for professions to be multiprofessional versus intraprofessional.[14] Multiprofessionalism involves each profession retaining specific knowledge and skills but being willing to collaborate with other professions. Interprofessionalism requires a willingness of professions to surrender work roles, to share knowledge, and to integrate procedures/treatments on behalf of the patient/client. The latter approach will be necessary as we enter the 21st century.

According to Carrier and Kendall, to succeed in this transition, the first question that must be answered is "For whose benefit is this being done?" The answer must be "for the patient/client."[15] Then professionals must be willing to share information and knowledge to best serve the patient. Many health professions assume a dominant role, being unwilling to relinquish boundaries. This posture serves to increase public and political scrutiny. However, to achieve interprofessionalism, professionals will need to become much more self-aware and confident.

In the athletic training profession, many steps have been taken recently to assure the viability of NATA and to prepare professionals for the future. The Education Task Force findings and recommendations of the mid-1990s (see Appendix B), the ongoing work of the Education Council, and the important work of the Research Foundation are instrumental in ensuring the best quality health care for athletes/clients and for ensuring that athletic training meets the conditions necessary to be a profession.

Some of the challenges facing athletic training include the following:

- Third party billing
- State licensure
- Education reform
- Increased research
- Advocacy
- Working conditions
- Diversifying

If we are to thrive as a profession, all athletic trainers must accept the responsibility to be aware of current issues and debates, to be involved in discussion and decision-making, and to provide support and input when it is solicited by state, district, and national leaders. There are critical windows of time when our participation is requested and needed. For example, when a state organization is proposing legislation for licensure or reclassification, all certified athletic trainers must take an active role in contacting legislators. Failure to be aware and involved could mean the difference between the advancement or the failure of the profession.

There are many other ways to be an advocate. Advocacy includes being consistent with the terms "athletic training" and "athletic trainer". We are not *trainers*, we are *athletic trainers*. Often athletic training is disguised (intentionally or not) with terms such as "sports medicine," "health services," or "sports science." This only serves to make the public confused about the terms and, even worse, takes away from the strength and pride of consistently using athletic training as the term for our profession (Figure 1-1).

Finally, the profession needs to change the working conditions of many practitioners. Working 60 to 80 hours per week in high school, clinic, and college settings for low compensation must be eradicated. To assist in the effort is the Appropriate Medical Coverage Task Force, which is researching the care provided to college athletes. As NATA president Kent Falb said in a January 1999 *NATA News* feature: "The time has come to correct the ever-increasing, unreasonable demands that have become commonplace in college settings."[16]

ATHLETIC TRAINING PROFESSION

Students are educated, role modeled, and socialized primarily in the college setting. Perpetuating the custom of working long hours (working hard) versus creating realistic, normal working hours (working smart) only serves to train yet another generation of students in the unfounded belief that "that is what it takes to be an athletic trainer." It also continues to reinforce to coaches and athletic administrators that athletic trainers are available at all times for no additional charge. Working smart versus working hard involves the following:

- Knowing how to organize
- Knowing the time required for each task
- Knowing how to evaluate what one is doing and making it more efficient while maintaining or improving quality

One can work hard in the sense of intensity during the working day, but not in the sense of long hours of time spent at work. Athletic trainers must begin to demand working hours and conditions that more accurately reflect those of a profession.

Figure 1-1. Students preparing for their future. Photograph by John Papa.

Professor T.S. Reeve,[17] speaking about the medical profession, says:

> "Unless we are committed to ensuring that we regulate ourselves and behave ethically, committed to imparting our knowledge and skills and to promoting research, and committed to excluding those who don't meet the standards, we are not acting as a proper body of professionals."

The athletic training profession faces a similar challenge, with the added responsibility of better informing other professionals and the public of who we are in a consistent and confident manner. We deserve equal standing with all other health/medical professions.

SUMMARY

Historically, there has never been a clear definition of the term "profession." The debate over definition continues into the 21st century as boundaries around professions became less distinct and more interdependent. At the heart of all professions is the upholding of a code of ethics.

To continue to be effective, professions need to begin sharing more information and skills to remain viable and offer patients the best possible care. Some of the many challenges that continue to face the athletic training professions in the 21st century include third party billing, state licensure, diversification, education reform, and advocacy for better working conditions in terms of working hours.

REFERENCES

1. Cruess RL, Cruess SR. Teaching medicine as a profession in the service of healing. *Acad Med.* 1997;72:941–952.

2. National Athletic Trainers' Association. *Athletic Training Educational Competencies.* Dallas, TX: National Athletic Trainers' Association; 1999.

3. Cogan ML. Toward a definition of profession. *Harvard Educational Review.* 1953;23:33–50.

4. Carr-Saunders AM. *Professions: Their Organization and Place in Society.* London: The Clarendon Press; 1928.

5. O'Shea ME. *A History of the National Athletic Trainers' Association.* Greenville, NC: National Athletic Trainers' Association; 1980.

6. Simpson J, Weiner E, eds. *The Oxford English Dictionary,* Vol 12. Oxford, UK: Clarendon Press; 1989.

7. Neufeldt V, ed. *Webster's New Word Dictionary of American English.* New York: Simon and Schuster; 1988.

8. Skeat W. *Etymological Dictionary of the English Language.* Oxford, Great Britain: Clarendon Press; 1963.

9. Freidson E. *Professionalism Reborn: Theory, Prophecy, and Policy.* Chicago, IL: The University of Chicago Press; 1994.

10. Moline JN. Professionals and professions: a philosophical examination of an ideal. *Soc Sci Med.* 1986;22:501–508.

11. Flexner SB, ed. *The Random House Dictionary of the English Language.* New York: Random House; 1987.

12. Cohen JJ. Breaking the mind mold. *Acad Med.* 1997;72:941–952.

13. Hilgenkamp K. Ethical behavior and professionalism in the business of health and fitness. *American College of Sports Medicine Health & Fitness Journal.* 1998;6:24–28.

14. Southon G, Braithwaite J. The end of professionalism? *Soc Sci Med.* 1998;46:23–28.

15. Carrier J, Kendall I. *Professionalism and Interprofessionalism.* London: Macmillan Press; 1993.

16. Falb K. Approach of new millennium necessitates changes. *NATA News.* 1999; January:12.

17. Reeve TS. The collegiate role in the development of professionalism in the modern community. *Aust NZ J Surg.* 1991;61:651–653.

Professionals and Ethics

"Knowledge is power."
Sir Francis Bacon

OBJECTIVES

On completion of this chapter, the student will be able to accomplish the following:

- Describe the four interrelated contexts that help develop a professional ethic
- Compare the similarities and differences of select health professions' codes of ethics
- Explain the process the National Athletic Trainers' Association uses to deal with violations of the code of ethics

PROFESSIONAL STANDARDS

As discussed in Chapter 1, professional organizations were developed to bring professionals together 1) to form an organized group, 2) to bring stronger recognition for their expertise, and 3) to create standards under which professionals operate. One of the hallmarks of a profession is its code of ethics—those standards and fundamental values that preserve the integrity of the profession, prevent misrepresentation among members, and protect against unethical practices or fraud. Members are expected to abide by these standards and policies and enforce ethical behavior among themselves.[1] Further, under the affective domain of

Professional Development and Responsibilities of the *Athletic Training Educational Competencies*,[2] there are competencies requiring an understanding of ethics (see Appendix A):

- Understands the consequences of noncompliance with regulatory athletic training practice acts
- Accepts the professional, historical, ethical, and organizational structures that define the proper roles and responsibilities of the certified athletic trainer in providing health care to athletes and others involved in physical activities
- Defends the moral and ethical responsibility to intervene in situations that conflict with National Athletic Trainers' Association (NATA) standards

CODES OF ETHICS

The word *ethic* comes from the Greek word *ethos*, which means the essence of one's character. We use the term to refer to the ultimate values and principles one holds. Amey and Reesor[3] refer to four interrelated contexts that help develop a professional's ethic: personal, institutional, professional, and legal. The personal ethic, which will be elaborated on in other chapters, refers to one's ultimate values, which are shaped by personal experiences and characteristics. The institutional ethic refers to the culture and policies of one's chosen workplace. The professional ethic has to do with expectations the profession (NATA) has of its members. The legal ethic is thought of in terms of legal considerations in forming one's ethic as well as an awareness of the increasingly litigious culture in which we live. This section examines the professional and institutional contexts in terms of the NATA code of ethics, differences and similarities among codes of ethics of select other health professions, and NATA's processes for complaints, disciplinary action, and appeals.

THE PROFESSIONAL CONTEXT

Every professional organization/association has its membership governed by a code of ethics. Professional codes of ethics have four primary purposes.[4] The professional code of ethics must provide direction—guidance for mandatory behavior by its members (these may also be highly recommended but not mandatory components in a profession's code of ethics). The code must be protective—it must protect the rights of athletes, patients, clients, subjects; their significant others; and the general public. The code must be specific—it must address areas of ethical issues and concerns particular to the discipline governed by the code. Finally, the code must be enforceable and enforced—the components of the codes must be observable and measurable (ie, "Is it occurring?" or "Is it not occurring?"). There must be a mechanism in place to ensure that all members are held to the standard and made to be accountable if they fail to meet the standard.

NATA's code of ethics was established in 1947, had major revisions in 1987, and has had several minor revisions since then, with the most recent in 1997. It contains both directive and recommended components (Table 2-1). The complete code can be found in Appendix C.

Statements in codes of ethics can be either *directive* or *nondirective*.[5] Most of the statements are directive (i.e., mandatory statements using the terms "shall" and "shall not"). Other statements are nondirective—made less rigid and stated as recommendations. For example, under the directive in Principle 2 ("Members shall comply with the laws and regulations governing the practice of athletic training"), Section 2.3 states: "Members are encouraged to report illegal or unethical practice pertaining to athletic training to the appropriate person or authority."

Another example of a recommendation rather than a mandate can be found under the directive in Principle 5 ("Members shall not engage in any form of conduct that constitutes a conflict of interest or that adversely reflects on the profession"), Section 5.1: "The private conduct of the member is a personal matter to the same degree as is any other person's except when such conduct compromises the fulfillment of professional responsibilities."

Several related codes of ethics will be presented here in order to gain a better perspective on our code and to understand the commonalities and differences among codes.

SELECT RELATED PROFESSIONAL CODES OF ETHICS

The American College of Sports Medicine (ACSM) code of ethics (Table 2-2) has four sections.

Table 2-1

NATIONAL ATHLETIC TRAINERS' ASSOCIATION CODE OF ETHICS: PREAMBLE

The Code of Ethics of the National Athletic Trainers' Association has been written to make the membership aware of the principles of ethical behavior that should be followed in the practice of athletic training. The primary goal of the Code is the assurance of high quality health care. The Code presents aspirational standards of behavior that all members should strive to achieve.

The principles cannot be expected to cover all specific situations that may be encountered by the practicing athletic trainer, but should be considered representative of the spirit with which athletic trainers make decisions. The principles are written generally and the circumstances of a situation will determine the interpretation and application of a given principle and of the Code as a whole. Whenever there is a conflict between the Code and legality, the laws prevail. The guidelines set forth in this Code are subject to continual review and revision as the athletic training profession develops and changes.

Principle 1: Members shall respect the rights, welfare, and dignity of all individuals.

Principle 2: Members shall comply with the laws and regulations governing the practice of athletic training.

Principle 3: Members shall accept responsibility for the exercise of sound judgment.

Principle 4: Members shall maintain and promote high standards in the provision of services.

Principle 5: Members shall not engage in any form of conduct that constitutes a conflict of interest or that adversely reflects on the profession.

National Athletic Trainers' Association, 1997. Reprinted with permission of the National Athletic Trainers' Association.

The first three are nondirective and stated as recommendations, using the verb "should" versus "shall." For example, Section 2 states: "Members should maintain high professional and scientific standards and should not voluntarily associate professionally with anyone who violates this principle."

The Guide for Professional Conduct of the American Physical Therapy Association (APTA; amended in 1996) serves to interpret the APTA code of ethics and matters of professional conduct (see Appendix D). Whereas most of the interpretation of this code is directive, some components are stated less directly as recommendations (using terms such as "should" or "may"). For example, under

Table 2-2

CODE OF ETHICS OF THE AMERICAN COLLEGE OF SPORTS MEDICINE

Principles and Purposes—Preamble: The principles are intended to aid Fellows and Members of the College individually and collectively to maintain a high level of ethical conduct. These are not laws but standards by which a Fellow or a Member may determine the propriety of his or her conduct and relationship with colleagues, with members of allied professions, with the public, and with all persons with whom a professional relationship has been established. The principal purpose of the College is the generation and dissemination of knowledge concerning all aspects of persons engaged in exercise with full respect for the dignity of man.

Section 1: Members should strive continuously to improve knowledge and skill and make available to their colleagues and the public the benefits of their professional attainment.

Section 2: Members should maintain high professional and scientific standards and should not voluntarily associate professionally with anyone who violates this principle.

Section 3: The College should safeguard the public and itself against members who are deficient in ethical conduct or professional competence.

Section 4: The ideals of the College imply that the responsibilities of each Fellow or Member extend not only to the individual, but also to society, with the purpose of improving both the health and well-being of the individual and the community.

Reprinted with permission from The American College of Sports Medicine.

Principle 3 ("Physical therapists accept responsibility for the exercise of sound judgment"), Section 3.3, Provision of Services, item D states: "In the event of elective termination of a physical therapist/patient relationship by the physical therapist, the therapist should take steps to transfer the care of the patient, as appropriate, to another provider."

Standards of ethical conduct for the physical therapist assistant were adopted by the APTA House of Delegates in June 1982 and can be found in Table 2-3. These standards are all directive.

There are many common threads running through these health care professions' codes. Chapter 1 explained that one of the hallmarks of a true profession is that it has a code of ethics. Another hallmark is that a true professional will always put the interest of his or her patient/client above his or her own personal gain. This prerequisite is evident in the codes presented. The commonalities among the examples

Table 2-3

STANDARDS OF ETHICAL CONDUCT FOR THE PHYSICAL THERAPIST ASSISTANT

Preamble: Physical therapy assistants are responsible for maintaining and promoting high standards of conduct. These Standards of Ethical Conduct for the Physical Therapist Assistant shall be binding on physical therapist assistants who are affiliate members of the Association.

Standard 1: Physical therapist assistants provide services under the supervision of a physical therapist.

Standard 2: Physical therapist assistants respect the rights and dignity of all individuals.

Standard 3: Physical therapist assistants maintain and promote high standards in the provision of services, giving the welfare of patients their highest regard.

Standard 4: Physical therapist assistants provide services within the limits of the law.

Standard 5: Physical therapist assistants make those judgements that are commensurate with their qualifications as physical therapist assistants.

Standard 6: Physical therapist assistants accept the responsibility to protect the public and the profession from unethical, incompetent, or illegal acts.

Adopted by the APTA House of Delegates, June 1982. Amended June 1991. Reprinted with permission from the American Physical Therapy Association.

given, as well as with other health care professions' codes of ethics, demonstrate that professions have overlap in their standards and values.

For example, NATA, ACSM, and APTA all have standards relating to protecting and respecting the rights of all individuals and promoting high standards in the provision of services.

Members of professional organizations assume the responsibilities and obligations set forth by their organization. When codes of ethics, policies, rules, standards, or by-laws are violated, the member is subject to sanctions ranging from a private reprimand to loss of certification and membership. The NATA Board of Directors investigates violations by using three panels: an Investigations Panel, a Fact-Finding Panel, and an Appellate (appeals) Panel.[6] Violations are reported to either NATA's Executive Director or the Chair of the Ethics Committee. The violations are investigated very carefully and methodically, with the member in question having an opportunity to appeal the charges. The proceedings are confidential. Should the member be found in violation of one or more standards, the sanctions levied may be made public. The Membership Sanctions and Procedures section of NATA's code of ethics can be found in Appendix E.

THE INSTITUTIONAL CONTEXT

The nature of any professional's work varies depending on the institution for which he or she works. New professionals (as well as more seasoned ones) are often remiss in making sure their personal ethics are congruent with the mission and vision of the institution where they seek employment. Athletic trainers, as professionals, have a responsibility to the institution. Practicing athletic trainers do not exist in a vacuum and do not operate exactly the same way without regard to whether the practice is in a clinical, industrial, university, high school, or other environment. One of the first tasks an athletic trainer should perform when assuming a new position is learn the history, the organizational structure and protocols, and the vision and mission of the place of employment. Other critical things to learn, such as internal and external politics, require an awareness over time and experience.

Athletic trainers do not work in isolation of the primary purpose of the institution. For example, those working in educational settings cannot ignore the fact that the primary purpose of the institution is to educate students, whereas in a clinical setting one of the purposes of the institution is to rehabilitate patients, perhaps provide medical services to the community, and, often, produce an annual profit. In an industrial setting, the institution's primary purpose may be to produce X number of quality products with a profit annually. It is imperative that one knows the mission of his or her employer. What may be an institutionally acceptable ethic in one type of employment setting may be grounds for dismissal at another. These institutional ethics, particularly in nontraditional environments, sometimes do not align with personal ethics, and one would be well-advised to find out as much background information as possible before accepting any job.

PROFESSIONAL INVOLVEMENT

Those who make the smoothest transition into professional practice are usually those whose personal ethics and priorities overlap and coincide with those of the chosen profession. It is vitally important for members of any profession to become involved in governance of the organization. For some, this involves active participation on local, state, district, or national committees; for others, it may involve keeping abreast of the issues, giving input when leaders are trying to make decisions that affect the future, and supporting the efforts of the various committees. Minimally, for any organization to survive and thrive, all members must know and understand the structure, the process of governance, the issues facing the profession, and, above all, exercise the right and privilege to vote. It goes without saying that to maintain membership, professionals must pay their annual membership fee in a timely fashion and, if certified, keep their continuing education units up to date.

SUMMARY

At the heart of all professional organizations is a code of ethics by which all members must abide. Standards or principles set forth in the code are mandatory and stated as directive. Subsections under each standard are sometimes stated as recommendations (nondirective) rather than directive. Members have a responsibility to intervene in situations that conflict with NATA standards. The NATA has a Membership Sanctions and Procedures section of the code of ethics, which handles any reported violations. Members have an obligation to understand the NATA structure and to be active in the process of governance by keeping abreast of current issues and exercising the right to informed vote.

REFERENCES

1. Hilgenkamp K. Ethical behavior and professionalism in the business of health and fitness. *Health and Fitness Journal.* 1998;6:24–28.

2. National Athletic Trainers' Association. *Athletic Training Educational Competencies.* Dallas, TX: National Athletic Trainers' Association; 1999.

3. Amey MJ, Reesor LM, eds. *Beginning Your Journey: A Guide for New Professionals in Student Affairs.* Washington, DC: National Association of Student Personnel Administrators; 1998.

4. Richardson ML, White KK. *Ethics Applied.* New York, NY: McGraw-Hill; 1993.

5. Scott R. *Professional Ethics: A Guide for Rehabilitation Specialists.* St. Louis, MO: Mosby; 1998.

6. National Athletic Trainers' Association. *Code of Ethics of the National Athletic Trainers' Association.* Dallas, TX: National Athletic Trainers' Association; 1997.

Chapter Three

Implications of Changing Environments

"In the end, it is important to remember that we cannot become what we need to be by remaining what we are."
Max DePree

OBJECTIVES

On completion of this chapter, the student will be able to accomplish the following:

- Differentiate among the characteristics of each generation of Americans in relation to the workplace
- Describe the challenges and opportunities Generation X brings to the workplace
- Explain the athletic trainer's role as a health care provider in a changing health care environment
- Recognize the multiskilling opportunities and advantages in today's workplace

Baseball great Yogi Berra's famous quote—"The future ain't what it used to be"—is appropriate in today's rapid-paced, constantly changing society. Nowhere is this more evident than in the health care field. The dynamic nature of the workplace can be viewed as threatening or opportunistic—threatening in the sense that things are not being done as they were in the past and employees must learn new skills to stay marketable; opportunistic in the sense that there is an open window that allows employees to be entrepreneurial and to diversify in ways never thought of before.

Under the affective domain of Professional Development and Responsibilities of the *Athletic Training Educational Competencies*,[1] at least one of the competencies relates to this phenomenon (see Appendix A):

- Appreciates the dynamic nature of issues and concerns as they relate to the health care of athletes and others involved in physical activity

In addition to changing health care and legislative issues, there is a changing workplace dynamic, with employees from very different generational upbringings and expectations working together. To be effective in the workplace, it is necessary to understand the people who comprise the workplace in the 21st century as well as the effect of a changing health care environment on athletic training.

Societal Changes

A host of information is available on the different generations and their goals and expectations. It is worthwhile to take a brief look at their general characteristics to understand better the philosophies and potential conflicts among different generations. Table 3-1 lists the generations and birth dates of those with the most potential to be in the current workplace.

Silent Generation

This group was preoccupied with world wars and a depression. People from this birth cohort are hard workers, loyal to their place of employment, and expect others to have a strong work ethic and to put the company's success ahead of personal needs. They believe nothing should ever be wasted and that procedures and policies are firmly set with repercussions for breaking them.

Baby Boomers

The baby boomers grew up in an opportune postwar environment where one could live the American Dream. Everyone was entitled to at least a middle class life, college enrollments escalated, and there were plenty of jobs and opportunities to go around. In the workplace, this generation believed that to advance you simply worked hard. They also believed, unlike the silent generation, that they

Table 3-1

WORKPLACE-AGE GENERATIONS OF AMERICANS

Generation	Birth Years*	Age in 2000, y
Silent Generation	1925–1942	58–75
Baby Boom Generation	1943–1960	40–57
Thirteenth Generation (Generation X)	1961–1981	19–39
Millennial Generation	1982–	18 and under

*Dates are approximate and vary by 2–4 years, depending on sources.

deserved to spend time and money on luxury items and to live in comfort. They were unconventional, rebellious, pragmatic, and hopeful.[2] This group created the greatest social movements and protests in US history.

Generation X (The Thirteenth Generation)

Generation X was born into an environment where Americans were deeply entrenched in being entitled to luxury and grew up with powerful images of comfort and style to live up to.[3] Generation X has observed powerful contradictions between a glossy, seemingly perfect life (their parents) and an increasingly growing level of homelessness, poverty, and job uncertainty. Diminishing economic opportunity is the basis for fear and uncertainty among this generation. In the workplace, Generation X employees (soon to be managers) have caused many employers to rethink their management styles and be creative in ways to motivate workers (Figure 3-1).

Generation X (which includes many young professionals and students) is a work force whose work values and ethic are very different from the ethic and values of other generations. It is imperative that Generation X understand the other generations and vice versa if everyone's potential is to be maximized in the workplace.

Generation X has experienced major changes in nearly all aspects of their lives— for instance, in family, childhood, gender roles, economic conditions and public policy, and technology advances. It was for this generation that the term "latchkey kids" was coined, and they did not spend their childhood in a single community— they moved around owing to parental job change or loss or change in their

Figure 3-1. Generation X students are independent, industrious, and resourceful. Photograph by John Papa.

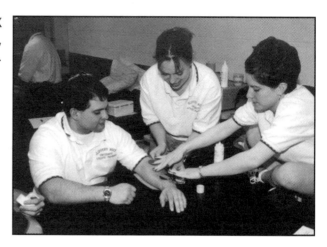

parents' marital status. As a result, the generation was hesitant to commit to long-term friendships and relationships and did not witness or experience enduring affiliations.[4] With funding for family programs and children diminishing (Generation X children have the distinction of being the most impoverished generation in America), politically, Generation X is much less interested in staying abreast of issues than earlier generations. Studies show that 56% of them feel a need to read the daily paper, versus 66% of late Boomers and 75% of early Boomers.[5]

Many reports reflect negative characteristics of Generation X. Table 3-2 lists the most commonly cited characteristics.[4]

It is important for Generation X professionals to recognize how their values and work ethic contrast with those of prior generational values and expectations. Generation X workers tend to resist loyalty to their workplace; they crave time and positive feedback from supervisors and want to learn new things. At the same time, they dislike disparaging remarks about their generation and inflexibility. They change jobs frequently (an average of once every 3.5 years).

This contrasts greatly with prior generations, who crave job security, value characteristics of punctuality and workplace loyalty, and understand corporate politics. Clearly both employers and employees must be aware of the differences and then focus on meeting needs, identifying positive attributes, finding commonalities, and seeking opportunities for innovation and creativity in the workplace.

Table 3-2

COMMON CHARACTERISTICS OF GENERATION X

- Self-absorbed and self-oriented
- Independent, industrious, and resourceful
- Value fun and balance in life
- Slow to commit to long-term relationships
- Extended adolescence—remain in parents' home and resist assuming adult roles
- Boomerang—leave but return to parents' home for economic reasons
- Marry late to avoid commitment or divorce
- Pluralistic and comfortable with diverse cultures and lifestyles
- Materialistic—practical, seasoned consumers
- Creative, decisive problem solvers
- Flexible, adaptable, and comfortable with change
- Voracious learners
- Parallel thinkers—able to do several things simultaneously
- Innovative risk takers and entrepreneurs
- Value quantity and quality time with significant adults
- Lack basic skills in reading, mathematics, and communication
- Cynical, pessimistic, practical, reality-driven worldview
- Unrealistic expectations for quick solutions to adult problems

Adapted from Kupperschmidt.[4]

HEALTH CARE MANAGEMENT

The last decade of the 20th century saw sweeping changes in health care. Health care is a business, and the business jargon, although still not comfortable to some, is here to stay. Health care management continues to involve downsizing, and the business world anticipates that white collar workers will be the next group affected.[6] Not only is health care being intensively managed, it is also being integrated. Mergers with similar institutions are occurring so rapidly that it is often hard to keep track of hospital and clinic names.

As health care is changing, the lines between professions are blending. More health care professionals have the same types of skills. In professional preparation, it is critical that students have an awareness of how their individual profession evolved historically. This gives one the ability to know how he or she is unique as an athletic trainer. We need to know how we, as professionals, are different. Athletic trainers need to know how they fit into the health care mix. Athletic training students need to know how to get a job over the next person with similar skills.

Part of the uniqueness is our professionalism—how we care for patients. The athletic trainer teaches and assists with prevention programs, handles injury properly when it occurs, and follows up with rehabilitation. In many instances, prevention programs are effective in minimizing the need for injury care and rehabilitation. The athletic trainer is one of the most unique physician extenders in health care.

The challenge to all athletic trainers is to realize our model of uniqueness as physician extenders and let the world know of our benefit. If we allow ourselves to blend too much (or call ourselves something different than we really are) we will go head-to-head with other health care professionals such as physical therapists or occupational therapists. As physician extenders, we are simply out in the working world doing what athletic trainers do—prevention, care, and rehabilitation.

To position yourself in the future, you must understand the health care trends of today. Health care management is here to stay—it is a business world, and it will affect what athletic trainers do. It cannot be ignored. In the area of rehabilitation, there is a very small dollar available. Many professions are competing for a piece of that small dollar. Our task is to know that we are unique and that we are professional in how we compete for our share.

MULTISKILLING AND CROSS-PROFESSIONAL TRAINING

With health care focused on containing costs and delivering services efficiently, there is an increasing interest in employees who can do more than one thing well. The 1995 Pew Health Professions Commission reports specifically recommended that allied health professional education programs focus on interdisciplinary care curricula and multiskilling: "Administrators are frustrated by single-skilled practitioners whose over-specialization results in under-utilization and cost increases, while the effective use of multiskilled allied health care practitioners has been well established over the past decade."[3]

Multiskilling is demonstrating competence in the skill sets of more than one health discipline. *Cross-professional training* is being prepared to perform functions associated with a different health care discipline.[7]

National Athletic Trainers' Association (NATA) Past-President Kent Falb challenged the profession in a feature article of the *NATA News* (October 1999): "Beginning today, we must make a pledge to diversify, individually and collectively. By doing so we have committed to our cornerstone of future achievements. Is diversification our failure? No. It is our future, absolutely."[8]

He goes on to say that legislation, reimbursement, and education reform has already occurred and we should expect to see changes in our practice setting: "Already we see this beginning. Athletic trainers now are working at rodeos, NASCAR races, figure skating rinks, ballet companies, firefighting services, and prisons."[8]

Multiskilling and cross-professional training in the health professions involve practice acts and ethical issues that will continue to be challenged and looked at well into the 21st century. Multiskilling in a broader context means acquiring skills above and beyond those required by one's certification. Certainly the athletic training credential can stand on its own, but in a very competitive job market, one can enhance job search success by adding skills. For example, owing to the aging population, one may want to add a minor in gerontology to an undergraduate degree. An emergency medical technician or paramedic certificate may open more doors. Any additional skills one can acquire or demonstrate in critical thinking or communication will make him or her a more versatile employee. Many students increase their skills by going to graduate school. Some students demonstrate their ability to be risk takers by participating in international study opportunities available at many universities. No one can forecast the future with precision, but it is certain that the job opportunities and requirements will be very different in the future than they are today.

THE GRADUATE SCHOOL DILEMMA

Currently, 41% of the 19,000 certified NATA members have or are completing a degree beyond the bachelor level. Most of these are master's degrees, with 1.4%

(270) certified members with doctorates. With the proliferation of newly certified members over the past 10 years, the percentage with advanced degrees has dropped considerably.

One of the toughest decisions facing most undergraduate athletic training students is whether to apply to graduate school, and if they decide in favor of this option, what to study and where. Athletic training faculty, staff, and others in authority offer varying philosophies to students, and often the advice is so divergent that the student ends up more confused than enlightened. This confusion could be for several reasons. First of all, the student is hearing many pieces of information that he or she may never have previously known. Until any volume of new information is digested and made sense of, most people tend to feel uncomfortable with it. Another cause for confusion or discomfort may be that the student holds several faculty, staff, or other authority figures in very high regard. If there is differing opinion (and often there is) from each authority, the student may perceive that to lean in one direction would offend one or more of his or her superiors. Finally, the student may simply feel overwhelmed at having to make the "right" decision from all the possible alternatives.

The following suggestions are offered as a guideline to navigate through the sea of opportunities. One needs to be a knowledgeable consumer. The first questions the student should ask are: "In what environment do I see myself eventually working?" and "What course of study/experiences will best serve to get me there?" Keep in mind that many other individuals will be vying for the same position, so you need to make sure you and your résumé stand out and are unique among all others. The prior section on multiskilling and cross-professional training offers some guidance in terms of what is currently marketable.

When choosing a graduate school, there are several questions worth investigating:

- Does the program I'm interested in have national recognition?
- Are graduate assistantships available?
- What is the placement rate for graduates (what percentage of graduates have a job when they graduate)?
- Are there faculty or staff who are nationally recognized as leaders/contributors to the profession? (This question is important because, whether one likes to admit it or not, it is often not what one knows but who one knows that opens doors for opportunities and jobs.)
- What specific courses are taught in the program? Do these courses add to my undergraduate foundation and will they prepare me for my future goals?

- Would the graduate assistantship give me an experience different than, or similar to, my undergraduate work?

Deciding what to major in is one of the most difficult decisions. Some questions and philosophies to think about hinge upon what environment one ultimately wants to work in. Whereas all possible scenarios cannot be addressed in this book, several common ones will be explored. For example, if one's ultimate goal is to one day teach in an athletic training curriculum program, it would be worthwhile to look at NATA-approved master's programs in athletic training to attain a more advanced knowledge base specifically in the field. It is clear that most institutes of higher education require a doctorate to be promoted to associate and full professor ranks. In fact, in the future, curriculum program directors will probably be required to have a doctorate. Another option for those interested in teaching in curricular programs is to complete a master's degree in a related field to broaden one's background and complete a doctoral degree with an athletic training emphasis. Some may argue that as long as one has a master's or doctorate degree in a related field (for example, education), one can teach in an athletic training curriculum. This may be true, but it should be remembered that one will teach students to come out of the undergraduate program knowing at least what he or she currently has learned. It would seem prudent to want to expand that knowledge and be at a more advanced level in the field of athletic training to be able to challenge the students.

Many students want to obtain a master's degree to make them more marketable for an athletic training job at the university level. If the division of intercollegiate athletics one wishes to work in is known, it would be wise to try to get experience as a graduate assistant in that environment. If one's undergraduate experience is already with that division, he or she might want to consider a higher division for a graduate assistantship or an assistantship working with a well-established mentor who could help open doors for those who can prove the quality of their work.

Another common dilemma occurs with entrepreneurial students who want to know what related profession would make them most marketable. Fortunately, certified athletic trainers have a broad enough health/medical background to enable them to branch off successfully in a multitude of professional directions. The more appropriate question is: "Which related health profession will make me most marketable in today's workplace?" (A caution: it is critical not to make a choice based solely on making more money and to choose a career path that will be enjoyed.) The unique skills an athletic trainer possesses can certainly stand on their own toe-to-toe with any profession. However, in a health care world that is extremely competitive, any professional is wise to consider multiskilling—adding credentials/skills that could make him or her more versatile and useful to more workplace environments. Currently, many students are looking toward combining their athletic training credentials with physician assistant, physical therapy, podiatry, exercise science, sport management, occupational therapy, nursing, or public school teaching credentials, to name a few.

Exciting opportunities are all around. Students need to give serious consideration to their interior "knowing" of what feels right for them for the future and then explore careers that fit within those boundaries. Sometimes a student will not know what seems right until he or she actually talks to someone or visits a particular program. The good news is that, no matter what related area is chosen, the student is versatile enough with an athletic training background to be successful.

SUMMARY

Differences in philosophy and expectations are occurring more frequently in the workplace as employees and employers increasingly come from different generational perspectives. It is important to take the time to recognize and understand these generational differences in order to create productive work environments. Rapidly changing health care, legislation, and education requirements dictate that athletic trainers prepare for a more diversified future. Multiskilling is necessary while we maintain and hold close those values and abilities that uniquely belong to athletic training. Diversifying means not only preparing individually to be more versatile, but also being on the outlook for more and varied venues in which to practice our profession.

REFERENCES

1. National Athletic Trainers' Association. *Athletic Training Educational Competencies.* Dallas, TX: National Athletic Trainers' Association; 1999.

2. Nelson R, Cowan J. *Revolution X.* New York, NY: Penguin Books; 1994.

3. Pew Health Professions Commission. *Critical Challenges: Revitalizing the Health Professions for the Twenty-First Century.* San Francisco, CA: UCSF Center for the Health Professions; 1995.

4. Kupperschmidt BR. Understanding generation X employees. *J Nurs Admin.* 1998;28:36–43.

5. Craig SC, Bennett SE, eds. *After the Boom: The Politics of Generation X.* Lanham, MD: Rowman and Littlefield Publishers; 1997.

6. Peters T. *Third Worldwide Lessons in Leadership Series Teleconference.* Boardman, OH, November 18, 1998.

7. Scott R. *Professional Ethics: A Guide for Rehabilitation Professionals.* St. Louis, MO: Mosby; 1998.

8. Falb K. Message from the president, SWATA Keynote address. *NATA News* 1999;36:14–16.

Chapter Four

Professional Preparation

"Our characters are the result of our conduct."
Aristotle

OBJECTIVES

On completion of this chapter, the student will be able to accomplish the following:

- Recognize the importance of mentors
- Identify ways to seek out mentors and mentoring opportunities
- Explain the role of networking in a professional's development
- Compare and contrast effective and noneffective time management skills

Students are given a very clear and extensive list of competencies in which they must show proficiency before being eligible to sit for the National Athletic Trainers' Association (NATA) Board of Certification examination. These competencies are divided into cognitive, psychomotor, and affective domains and are assessed in multiple ways by faculty, staff, and clinical instructors within academic programs. As stated in Chapter 1, affective competencies relevant to this text can be found in Appendix A. This chapter is relevant to several affective competencies in the *Athletic Training Educational Competencies*[1] under Health Care Administration:

- Respects the roles and cooperation of medical personnel, administrators, and other staff members in the organization and administration of athletic training service programs.

- Recognizes the certified athletic trainer's role as a liaison among athletes, physically active individuals, caretakers, employers, physicians, coaches, other health care professionals, and any individual who may be involved with the care provided by the certified athletic trainer.

Under Professional Development and Responsibilities:

- Respects the role and responsibilities of other health care professionals.

There is another set of skills and abilities that is much more difficult to define, teach, and assess, but that might well be the most critical determinant of a student's future success in the field. These are the student's personal characteristics—those qualities and abilities unique to each person in how he or she approaches situations, interacts with others, and takes in and processes information. This chapter will examine some of the professional and personal attributes necessary to develop a career in athletic training.

ROLE SOCIALIZATION

Role socialization refers to learning of social roles that facilitate participation and adequate professional performance in the society of which one is a member (in this case, the athletic training profession).[2] This includes the knowledge, skills, and dispositions (role demands) attached to the status of being an athletic trainer. The process of learning occurs in an interactional context and explicitly specifies for the student how other professionals will behave.[2] When asked if formal courses are sufficient to instill a sense of professionalism among medical students, Epstein[3] replied that they are not. He believes that a state of awareness called "mindfulness" is necessary and that the cultivation of mindfulness requires mentoring and guidance, not formal coursework. Ludmerer says that in the broad view of the professionalization process with medical students, "attitudes are shaped by the totality of students' interactions with faculty, house officers, patients, hospital staff, and one another in laboratories, classrooms, wards, and clinics."[4]

The process of socialization is very important, especially in the learning of interpersonal skills and dispositions. The following sections elaborate on specific skills that professionals must learn to be highly successful.

MENTORING

One of the most important tasks for the student is to identify someone in the NATA or a related profession to be a mentor. The term "mentor" is defined by *Webster's* as "a wise adviser; a trusted teacher and counselor."[5] A mentor is someone the student respects and who cares about the student's professional and personal growth. A mentoring relationship usually lasts for at least a year (often over longer periods of the student's life) as the student continues to develop throughout his or her career. These typically are not short-term (eg, over one weekend) relationships. It is critical to take the time to meet professionals in the field who the student can respect and to find ways to converse in order to determine if a particular individual shows an interest in the student as a developing professional.

Sometimes students do not take advantage of appropriate opportunities to sit beside an instructor or staff supervisor in informal situations (a bus ride, a slow time at the office or during office hours, while watching a competition) to ask questions and to learn more. Some students fear being labeled a "teacher's pet" by their peers, which is unfortunate, as during the formal education years (both graduate and undergraduate) one has more immediate access to "experts" in the athletic training field than in almost any other setting (Figure 4-1).

Understanding the diverse backgrounds, experiences, and philosophies of all faculty and staff members can be invaluable if one chooses to make the commitment to learn all that is possible from them. This has nothing to do with formal class or clinic work. It has everything to do with some of the rich history each professional possesses—experiences and knowledge that class and clinic requirements simply do not afford the time to explore. The only way to access this very important component of the educational process is by having an awareness of the appropriate time and place to approach an individual and the initiative to do it. There are several tips to help balance the approach to a mentor, including the following[6]:

1. Clarify needs and expectations—mentors have certain strengths, but will probably not be able to meet all needs.
2. Be time conscious—mentors are busy people who will value the relationship, but be respectful of their schedules and do not become a burden.
3. Create a dialogue—it is important to know when to talk and when to be a good listener.

Figure 4-1. Mentors play a key role in student development. Photograph by John Papa.

4. Foster respect and appreciation—while seeking someone to support and care about one's career development, it is necessary to show the same respect for the mentor.

Mentoring experience opportunities exist in almost every setting to which one is exposed as a student athletic trainer. These are times—in classrooms, clinical, and other professional preparation environments—when the student has the opportunity to watch what is going on and what people do. Simply recognizing a situation as a mentoring experience and just being aware of what is happening requires one to "be" in situations differently. If one is aware and paying attention to what is going on, he or she will find many role models in action. One other way of finding a mentor is through effective networking.

NETWORKING

"Networking" means creating and maintaining connections with professionals inside and outside the workplace. It also means being involved and connected. It has a negative connotation for some people, who may think it sounds manipulative and artificial or consider it in terms of "the old boys' network," where gaining favors, loyalties, or personal influence are operating. However, networking with the intent to connect with professionals and new colleagues through a collaborative, collegial process is an important and necessary part of becoming a contributing professional. Networking not only assists individuals, it enhances a profession by encouraging competence, communication, and support.[7]

Pancrazio and Gray[7] use the following definition of network: "(It) increases the probability of success for its individual members in numerous ways. It acts as an employment service. It gives members useful professional, social, and political contacts, thus expanding their bases of influence . . . A network also provides members mutually beneficial psychological and economic support."

Helfgott[8] echoes similar values of networking, saying it can help to "increase your level of confidence; acquire mentors; tap into the 'hidden' job market; exchange valuable information, knowledge, resources, and contacts; give and receive advice and moral support; form long-term personal and professional relationships."

Networking is not an organizational "bottom-up" or "top-down" issue. There may be advantages and value to making connections with persons at higher levels, but equally as valuable are the contacts and connections made with peers and colleagues in other departments within the organization. These connections can often make the student and his or her colleagues more successful in their own positions. For example, making a sincere point to get to know people in the counseling, financial, personnel, facility, or custodial departments to gain a mutual understanding is an enriching experience. Often this groundwork of mutual respect will go a long way if one has to deal with a conflict or problem involving this networked colleague's department in the future or if assistance requiring his or her expertise is needed. Above all, be sure to be genuine and sincere in these relationships versus just networking for networking's sake. To do otherwise for nonauthentic reasons would be manipulative and not in the true spirit of developing a useful network. If one is only trying to make artificial contacts and use people or enter the relationship with a "what's in it for me" mentality, he or she is not networking. A sincere interest in someone's background, values, thoughts, and opinions is the foundation of networking.[6]

> "Hold onto what is good
> Even if it is a handful of earth
> Hold onto what you believe in
> Even if it is a tree which stands by itself
> Hold onto what you must do
> Even if it is a long way from here
> Hold onto life
> Even if it is easier to let go
> Hold onto my hand
> Even when I have gone away from you"   Pueblo Indian Poem

LEADERSHIP

Leadership can be defined in many ways. In the professional development context, all athletic trainers need to possess leadership skills in order to persuade others to work toward a common goal. This may occur during one-on-one interaction with athletes or when contributing as a member of staff, a committee, or a project team. Leadership also means being supportive of others as they carry out their tasks. An effective leader uses a participatory management style, allowing team members to have input, based on mutual respect and trust.[9]

Professionals must develop the initiative and leadership skills that involve supporting (empowering) peers and colleagues. This includes creating an environment that promotes opportunities and demonstrating a willingness to "roll up your sleeves" and get involved with helping others achieve. One of the most effective ways to influence others' behavior is to lead by example.

Emotional intelligence has recently emerged as a strong component in what makes people develop into exceptional professionals. Daniel Goleman, a leading author on the subject, purports that it is not usually the most intelligent person who is the most able in any organization. Often, it is the modestly intelligent who perform at superior levels. Emotional intelligence has to do with self-control, zeal, and persistence. Persons with these characteristics will become "stars" in any organization, and these attributes can be learned. "For star performance, in all jobs, in every field, emotional competence is twice as important as cognitive abilities."[10]

In terms of leadership, Goleman believes that to be maximally effective, self-control and compassion are needed—that is, intellect and heart. Without these qualities, one will not get optimal results from the individual or group with which he or she is working. Being able to bring a committee or project team together to work harmoniously involves leadership skills that are very much like effective coaching or educator skills.

Certainly, personal characteristics, knowing how to organize, and understanding of the time requirements of various tasks are also important leadership qualities. There are volumes of books written on leadership, but these basic concepts, which can be learned, will help achieve goals that are for the common good. Those who are interested in becoming leaders of organizations or assuming administrative roles may want to attend workshops or classes on leadership and management, strategic planning, or finances. Networking and finding a mentor in a leadership role is invaluable.

CHARACTER

Character comes from the Greek verb meaning "to engrave" and its related noun meaning "mark" or "distinctive quality." Character evolves and can be developed.

"Character is the sum total of all those morally relevant habits that we have developed. It is also the source of our most immediate, as well as our most reflective, responses to the world."[11]

Sommers[12] indicates that the basics of good character include civility, honesty, consideration, and self-discipline. The United States Senate bill designating a National Character Counts! Week defines the core elements of character as trustworthiness, respect, responsibility, fairness, caring, and citizenship. These are also the core elements of what constitutes a professional. A person's character is the permanent and visible sign of his or her inner nature. The signs can be acts, words, or the failure to act or speak. For example, if you were on a road trip and observed an athlete steal a glass from a dinner table, what would you do? Would you turn away and pretend not to see it (failure to act or speak) or would you confront the athlete or inform the coach of the act?

ORGANIZATION AND TIME MANAGEMENT

Entry level athletic trainers usually come into the workplace possessing strong skills in time management, organization, and goal setting. The undergraduate athletic training curriculum (demanding coursework and many challenging clinical hours) requires students to learn to balance their lives, set clear priorities, and manage their time carefully. It would be difficult to graduate from a program without possessing some of these skills. These skills, with a few adjustments, can be transferred to the workplace easily.

A prior chapter alluded to the importance of organization and time management in working smarter and more effectively. The time spent organizing materials, files, procedures, and thoughts will be more than offset by the positive benefits reaped later. Disorganization can lead to chaos when sudden changes or emergencies arise and one is unprepared to respond.

One of the first places to begin organizing is in the daily schedule. Every student or professional should have a calendar or monthly planner that allows him or her to note key events/appointments/meetings for each day and the ability to look at future weeks and months for upcoming events. Another helpful organization tool is a "to do" list—a weekly or daily list created to be sure the most important items that need attention are not forgotten. Be sure to put personal time for exercise, reflection, reading, and time with significant others on the weekly list. Making time to take care of yourself will make you much more effective in dealing with work situations. Too often, athletic trainers, as well as other professionals involved with caring for others, do not make this a priority. There are many stressors that student athletic trainers may be dealing with on a typical day—for example, an examination, a team with many injuries and not enough time or modality availability to get them ready for practice, lack of sleep, illness, family problems, or financial concerns. As with leadership, many texts are written on the importance of organization and how to create a more organized workplace. Taking time to care for oneself (spiritually and physically) can be assisted by using the many stress management and relaxation books, tapes, and classes available.

Time management is another component of organization. Consider these quotes:

"The more a person is able to direct his life consciously, the more he can use time for constructive benefits."   Rollo May

"Time is the scarcest resource and unless it can be managed, nothing else can be managed."   Peter Drucker

"We are what we do with our time."   Benjamin Franklin

There are potentially many events that can absorb time on a daily basis (such as crises, telephone, e-mail, correspondence/reading, procrastination, unexpected visitors, meetings). If one does not learn to prioritize and determine what is really important, he or she can spend the entire day doing unexpected, unplanned things and feel like he or she has no control over what has happened. This can create a victimized, stressful feeling; however, it is preventable. Awareness of what is going on is the first step, followed by a few simple rules to help one to work smarter, not harder. Remember, everyone has 168 hours per week—no more, no less. The goal is to make more *effective* use of time, not more efficient use of time (although this will probably occur).

In Alan Lakein's best-seller *How to Get Control of Your Time and Your Life*,[13] he discusses the following strategies to make life less complicated. To establish goals and priorities, make a "to do" list for daily activities (preferably the night before, but try to make it the same time each day). Keep the list simple and, most importantly, realistic. Prioritize the list, noting top priorities with As, lowest priorities with Cs, and the rest with Bs. Now select the one top priority as A-1. The goal here is not to cross off as many activities in the day as possible, but to use time more effectively.

Categorizing according to the following can help in selecting A, B, or C categories:

- Important and urgent
- Important but not urgent
- Urgent but not important
- Busywork marginally worth doing

A few strategies (such as learning to say "no" to urgent but not important interruptions during the day; checking your e-mail or voice messages only once or twice a day at a set time; honestly telling drop-ins that you really want to talk with them, but could they return in 1 hour) can help you stay in control of time and allow tasks to be completed.

The following three techniques might also prove useful:

The 80/20 Principle[13]
- 80% of everything in the world are Cs—don't spend more than 20% of time on them
- On a list of 10 "to do" items, only two will yield the greatest amount of professional and personal satisfaction. Find them, make them As, and focus efforts on them
- Leave the Cs until the end

Ask "What is the best use of my time right now?"
- Decide quickly
- Ask "What will happen if I don't do the Cs?"
- Put C items in a file out of sight
- Keep As and Bs in separate files and do accordingly

Handling Paper
- After sorting, handle only once
- Do not pick up a piece of paper unless you intend to do something with it and have the time to do so

- Write answers on incoming mail
- Keep background reading material (eg, journals) in a separate pile
- Get off mailing and e-mail lists
- Stop paper-shuffling

A professor at a major university had the following sign on his door: *"Lack of planning on your part does not constitute an emergency on mine."* In other words, be careful not to get caught up and take ownership of other people's As at the expense of your own.

Knowing how to organize the day and week and how to manage time is part of developing into a mature professional. Fortunately, one of the strengths of most athletic trainers is their ability to handle multiple things at one time. We are not just record-keepers; rehabilitation, prevention, and care of injury specialists; liaisons with insurance companies; advocates with parents; administrators; or supplies and budget stewards. We do all of these things as well as serve on committees, lead projects, and mentor others. We are well-trained to handle this diverse array of responsibilities on a daily basis.

Remember that you can really only do one thing well at a time—give it full attention and then go on to the next thing. If organization and time management are areas where you can improve, consider trying one of the aforementioned strategies for a week to begin improving efficiency and productivity.

SUMMARY

Preparing to be a professional involves much more than the NATA required courses and clinical experiences. It requires an awareness of the personal characteristics you possess and how you use them to interact with others. Being open to new ideas, being willing to change, and having the ability to work harmoniously with others are not easily measured, but are critically important in programs that strive for excellence. To survive in the 21st century workplace, it is important to develop and nurture networking, leadership, and time management skills. It is also important to recognize personal needs and limitations and take the necessary time to restore energy levels via stress management techniques or relaxation.

REFERENCES

1. National Athletic Trainers' Association. *Athletic Training Educational Competencies*. Dallas, TX: National Athletic Trainers' Association; 1999.

2. Hardy M, Conway M. *Role Theory*. East Norwalk, CT: Appleton & Lange, 1988.

3. Epstein RM. Mindful practice. *JAMA*. 1999;282:833–839.

4. Ludmerer KM. Instilling professionalism in medical education. *JAMA*. 1999; 282:881–882.

5. Neufeldt V, ed. *Webster's New Word Dictionary of American English*. New York, NY: Simon & Schuster; 1988.

6. Reesor L. Making professional connections. In: Amey M, Reesor L, eds. *Beginning Your Journey*. Washington, DC: National Association of Student Personnel Administrators; 1998.

7. Pancrazio S, Gray R. Networking for professional women: a collegial model. *Journal of National Association of Women Deans Administrators and Counselors*. 1982; 45:16–19.

8. Helfgott D. Take 6 steps to networking success. *Planning Job Choices: 1995*. Bethlehem, PA: College Placement Council; 1995.

9. Thomas C, Correa V, Morsink C. *Interactive Teaming: Consultation and Collaboration in Special Programs*. Englewood Cliffs, NJ: Prentice Hall; 1995.

10. Goleman D. *Working with Emotional Intelligence*. New York, NY: Bantam Books; 1998.

11. Morris T. *If Aristotle Ran General Motors: The New Soul of Business*. New York, NY: Henry Holt and Company; 1997.

12. Sommers C. What college students don't know. In: Josephson MS, Hanson W, eds. *The Power of Character*. San Francisco, CA: Jossey-Bass; 1998.

13. Lakein A. *How to Get Control of Your Time and Your Life*. Bergenfield, NJ: The New American Library; 1973.

Chapter Five

Professional Decision-Making

"This above all, to thine own self be true, and it must follow as the night
the day, thou canst not then be false to any man."
William Shakespeare

OBJECTIVES

On completion of this chapter, the student will be able to accomplish the following:

- Define critical thinking
- Explain how to use an analytical approach to defending or asserting an argument
- Define metacognition and explain ways to use it to check the rigor of any analysis
- Describe the "truth and consequences" of whistle-blowing

In all health disciplines, professionals must have the ability to make independent decisions and judgments within the domains of their practice. The National Athletic Trainers' Association (NATA) code of ethics states, "Members shall accept responsibility for the exercise of sound judgment" (Principle 3). Ethical decision making, whether in clinical, educational, research, school, home, or other settings, requires careful compliance with professional, institutional, and legal standards and mandates.[1] Sometimes these standards are in conflict and this creates serious dilemmas for the health professional. Under the affective domain of Health Care

Administration in the *Athletic Training Educational Competencies*,[2] the following competency relates to the need for sound decision-making (see Appendix A):

- Recognizes and accepts the need for organizing and conducting health care programs for athletes and other physically active individuals on the basis of sound administrative policies and procedures.

Ethical decision-making models for health care professionals governing patient care are based on four foundational biomedical ethical principles: beneficence, nonmaleficence, justice, and autonomy.[1] *Beneficence* is acting in the patient's best interest—athletic trainers are the athletes' fiduciaries (ie, they stand in a position of special trust and confidence). *Nonmaleficence* means professionals are bound not to intentionally harm patients under their care. *Justice* means treating all persons equally. *Autonomy* means respecting and acknowledging that all patients have the right of self-determination (particularly in treatment decision-making). Hospitals and many other health care facilities publicly display a Patient Bill of Rights and Responsibilities to ensure that patients know their rights and responsibilities.

PROBLEM-SOLVING AND JUDGMENT

Athletic trainers make decisions on a daily basis regarding athlete care, staffing, administrative duties, institutional protocol, and factors affecting their personal lives. Sometimes situations are urgent and these decisions must be made rapidly; other times, there may be hours, days, weeks, or months to gather facts to make an informed decision. Regardless of the time frame, sound, unbiased decisions should be made using a set of skills and abilities. This section of the chapter will deal with identifying these skills and abilities and realizing that they can be learned. Then the learner must be willing, not just able, to make informed, skilled, and fair-minded judgments as he or she solves problems, makes decisions, and engages in professional practice.[3]

Nationally, many professions have identified critical thinking as one of the essentials to knowledge development, professional practice, and an educated public. Former President George Bush's National Goals for Education for the year 2000 also identified critical thinking as essential. In 1990, the American Philosophical Association released conclusions made by consensus by an expert group of philosophers regarding the definition, skills, and dispositions of critical

Table 5-1

CRITICAL THINKING COGNITIVE SKILLS AND SUBSKILLS

Skills	Subskills
Interpretation	Categorization Decoding sentences Clarifying meaning
Analysis	Examining ideas Identifying arguments Analyzing arguments
Evaluation	Assessing claims Assessing arguments
Inference	Querying evidence Conjecturing alternatives Drawing conclusions
Explanation	Stating results Justifying procedures Presenting arguments
Self-Regulation	Self-examination Self-correction

Adapted from Facione.[4]

thinking.[4] Critical thinking is defined as "purposeful, self-regulatory judgement which results in interpretation, analysis, evaluation, and inference."[4] Table 5-1 further defines the skills and subskills necessary to make sound judgments.

The Third Report of the Pew Health Professions Commission[5] stated, "All allied health practitioners will be expected to have a strong foundation in the sciences, increased critical thinking and problem-solving skills, and excellent communication abilities" (Figure 5-1).

Perhaps an even more useful definition from the American Philosophical Association Delphi Report (in terms of athletic trainer clinical judgment) is the disposition profile of an ideal critical thinker.[4] A "disposition" can be defined as an inclination or a desire to seek out opportunities to use or do certain things. In this case, there are several abilities that have been defined as necessary to develop to be a good thinker and decision-maker:

Figure 5-1. Students engaged in peer problem-solving. Photograph by John Papa.

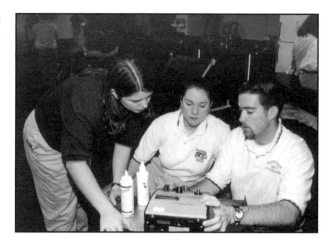

"The ideal critical thinker is habitually inquisitive, well-informed, honest in facing personal biases, prudent in making judgments, willing to reconsider, clear about issues, orderly in complex matters, diligent in seeking relevant information, reasonable in the selection of criteria, focuses in inquiry, and persistent in seeking results which are as precise as the subject and the circumstances of inquiry permit."[4]

Facione and Facione have defined seven dispositions inherent in the Delphi Report (Table 5-2).[6] Content knowledge and strong thinking skills are essential in today's rapidly changing world, yet they are insufficient. Facione et al state that "To go beyond the minimum, workers, learners, and citizens must be willing and able to critique intelligently and amend judiciously the methods, conceptualizations, contexts, evidence, and standards applied in any given problem situation."[3] The challenge for mentors, educators, and students is to prepare graduates who are both able and willing to think.

To summarize, people may have the knowledge of a topic and the skill to think well, but unless it is demanded of them by some external force, they may not engage the problem and actually apply their skills. In other words, if they are not disposed (or motivated) to use critical thinking, they will not use thinking as their primary problem-solving strategy. Rather, they will rely on habitual or rehearsed strategies, which may or may not result in the best solutions.

Students can enhance their own critical thinking/problem-solving abilities by approaching problems with an analytical focus. For example, in making an argu-

Table 5-2

THE DISPOSITION TOWARD CRITICAL THINKING: SEVEN FACTOR ANALYSIS

Factor	Definition
Truthseeking	A courageous desire for the best knowledge, even if such knowledge fails to support or undermines one's preconceptions, beliefs, or self-interests
Open-mindedness	Tolerance to divergent views, self-monitoring for possible bias
Analyticity	Demanding the application of reason and evidence, alert to problematic situations, inclined to anticipate consequences
Systematicity	Valuing organization, focus, and diligence to approach problems of all levels of complexity
Critical Thinking Self-confidence	Trusting of one's own reasoning skills and seeing oneself as a good thinker
Inquisitiveness	Curiosity and eagerness to acquire knowledge and learn explanations even when the applications of the knowledge are not immediately apparent
Maturity	Prudence in making, suspending, or revising judgment; an awareness that multiple solutions can be acceptable; an appreciation of the need to reach closure even in the absence of complete knowledge

Adapted from Facione.[6]

ment for or against a particular issue, or in responding to assertions made by someone else, consider the following[7]:

- What is the issue and what are the key concepts/relationships central to the issue?
- Is the person (or are you) making any underlying assumptions?
- Are there any secondary arguments or claims being advanced?

- Is there any evidence for the validity of the claims being made?
- Are there alternative arguments, positions, or strategies that could be advocated?
- Is there justification for the position or stance taken based on your analysis?
- Is the professional position taken important enough to pursue?

It is easy to simply make a response and not take the time to look carefully at what the issues are. No matter how many times one has dealt with a similar problem, every time is different, and taking the time to focus on the issues, not recite a rehearsed reply, is critical. A very important part of being an effective thinker is the ability to reflect on one's own thinking processes. This is known as *metacognition*. Facione and Facione[7] suggest that individuals and groups check the rigor of their analysis using the following metacognitive questions:

- Are we open to new ideas even if they fail to support our preconceptions, beliefs, or self-interests?
- Are we being tolerant to divergent views?
- Are we demanding the application of reason and evidence?
- Are we anticipating the consequences of the arguments we espouse?
- Are we being focused and diligent in our approach to the issue(s)?
- Are we being prudent in making, suspending, or revising our judgments; considering multiple solutions; and coming to closure on an issue when necessary?

The ability to create or analyze an argument objectively and logically is a powerful tool for a young professional. It is often easier to present ideas or responses from a habitual opinion-based perspective, but it is far more effective to take the time to check out one's intentions and biases and seek the truth, wherever it leads. This takes courage and self-confidence and leads to professional growth.

WHISTLE-BLOWING

An issue of conflicting obligations involves what is known as "whistle-blowing." Whistle-blowing is the term used when one exposes a colleague who is incompetent or unethical. This can create a conflict between obligations to society and obligations to support professional colleagues. There are laws in some states to protect whistle-blowers.

If confronted with this type of situation, what is the best approach to take? The whistle-blower must live with the ramifications. Going along with something one does not believe in can make him or her miserable; whistle-blowing can make one stand alone and could ruin a career—but the person's conscience is clear.

Most codes of ethics contain guidelines about protecting the integrity of the profession. The NATA code of ethics states: "Members are encouraged to report illegal or unethical practice pertaining to athletic training to the appropriate person or authority." The American Medical Association's Principles of Medical Ethics states "A physician shall . . . strive to expose those physicians deficient in character or competence, or who engage in fraud or deception." The American Physical Therapy Association Code of Ethics and Guide for Professional Conduct states "Physical therapists shall report any conduct that appears to be unethical, incompetent, or illegal." Other health profession codes contain similar language.

The reality of exposing an incompetent or unethical colleague is much more daunting than it appears in reading a code of ethics. It could be a lose-lose situation—the colleague may lose his or her job; other colleagues may distrust the whistle-blower. It may be difficult to blow the whistle, even when professionally the code has been broken, for several reasons[8]:

1. The individual may be a friend.
2. You may believe it is none of your business.
3. You may be able to rationalize the individual's behavior to yourself.

Whistle-blowing is a courageous step to undertake, and one that is necessary to uphold professional standards. Above all, remember the following:

1. To thine own self be true—if a breach of conduct has occurred, your inner self will need to live with a decision not to report it.
2. When whistle-blowing is done with integrity and respect, exposure upholds the dignity of the patient and of the profession.

Remember also that the whistle-blower is not responsible for the outcome of the individual involved. There are procedures in place for disciplinary bodies of professions to handle these situations in a professional and equitable way. The NATA procedures were discussed in Chapter 2 and are located in Appendix C.

SUMMARY

Most health care professionals have determined critical thinking ability to be essential for success in the field. Athletic trainers make many decisions on a daily basis. It is worthwhile to think about how you would engage a problem and its solution. Often the solution is rehearsed and based on past decisions or stances without revisiting the problem to see if there might be another acceptable solution. Asking a set of questions that causes you to reflect on your own thinking (metacognition) is an effective way to avoid rehearsed, habitual answers.

A delicate area that requires sound professional decision-making is whistle-blowing. This involves an athletic trainer (or any employee) in conflicting obligations—that to the society of professionals you represent and that to support a professional colleague. Several pros and cons must be analyzed and in the end the athletic trainer must be able to live with his or her conscience. Fortunately, there are procedures in place in the NATA Membership Sanctions and Procedures to assist with this type of decision.

The ability to make good professional judgments and engage in sound decision-making involves a set of skills and abilities that can be learned if the student is willing to work toward that goal.

REFERENCES

1. Scott R. *Professional Ethics: A Guide for Rehabilitation Professionals.* St. Louis, MO: Mosby; 1998.

2. National Athletic Trainers' Association. *Athletic Training Educational Competencies.* Dallas, TX: National Athletic Trainers' Association; 1999.

3. Facione P, Facione N, Giancarlo C. The motivation to think in working and learning. In: Jones E, ed. *Defining Expectations for Student Learning.* San Francisco, CA: Jossey-Bass; 1997.

4. Facione P. Critical thinking: a statement of expert consensus for purposes of educational assessment and instruction. In: *The Delphi Report: Research Findings and Recommendations Prepared for the American Philosophical Association* (ERIC Doc. No. ED315-423). Washington, DC: ERIC; 1990.

5. Pew Health Professions Commission. *Critical Challenges: Revitalizing the Health Professions for the Twenty-First Century.* San Francisco, CA: UCSF Center for the Health Professions; 1995.

6. Facione N, Facione P. Externalizing critical thinking in knowledge development and clinical judgment. *Nursing Outlook*. 1996;44:129–36.

7. Facione N, Facione P. *Teaching and Measuring CT: Preparing Students for Professional Challenges*. Millbrae, CA: The California Academic Press; 1993.

8. Parsons PH, Parsons AH. *Health Care Ethics*. Middletown, OH: Wall & Emerson; 1992.

Chapter Six

Communication Skills:
The Key to Success

"Communication is simply mutual understanding."
Stephen R. Covey

OBJECTIVES

On completion of this chapter, the student will be able to accomplish the following:

- Distinguish between effective and non-effective verbal and nonverbal professional communication
- Explain the importance and implications of understanding how individuals take in and process information
- Explain the importance of cultural sensitivity in health care environments
- Identify several sources of information regarding cultural practices of specific countries

Two of the affective competencies under the Psychosocial Intervention and Referral section of the *Athletic Training Educational Competencies*[1] have relevance to this chapter:

- Accepts the need for appropriate interpersonal relationships between all of the parties involved with athletes and others involved in physical activity
- Respects the various social and cultural attitudes, beliefs, and values regarding health care practices when caring for athletes

Figure 6-1. Development of strong communication skills is imperative. Photograph by John Papa.

The value of developing strong communication skills cannot be overstated. Communication style tells the receiver(s) a great deal about the communicator. Often it is not what is said but how it is said that influences others' reactions to and impressions of the speaker. Communication consists of many components, including oral, written, nonverbal, and computer technology. Use of proper grammar, voice projection, and congruence in what we say (ie, what we say is true and represents our beliefs) will be noticed by our audience (Figure 6-1).

At the basis of all effective communication is an attitude component that serves as a type of paradigm—a way of thinking about communicating and approaching people. Dr. James Laux, Associate Professor of Communication at Slippery Rock University, espouses this belief and has a theory about "communicating with CARE," an acronym that stands for a cluster of skills and knowledge (Table 6-1). He talks to his classes about the greatest rule: "Love thy neighbor as thyself." Every major religious group ascribes to a similar rule. This is the fundamental element of all interpersonal communication, both professional and personal. It must be present for genuine effectiveness. For example, if one attends a workshop on effective listening, he or she can learn the skills and steps necessary to become an effective listener. However, when one goes out into the world with a personal or professional approach that does not include this caring philosophy, listening skills will come across as artificial, contrived, or superficial. Genuine and effective communication is characterized by the attitude espoused in CARE.

Relationships are fundamentally important in life. There is a sacredness—an essence—in others, and to be truly effective one needs to encounter them at that level.

Table 6-1

COMMUNICATING WITH CARE

C—Clarity

A—Authenticity

R—Responsiveness

E—Empathy

Created by Dr. James Laux, Associate Professor of Communication, Slippery Rock University.

Clarity and authenticity are expressive skills; responsiveness and empathy are receptive skills. Communication, in a fundamental way, is a reciprocal process of giving and receiving. At times, it may be best to turn CARE around and communicate with ERAC, to listen with empathy, respond, assert one's own ideas, and clarify anything that is misunderstood. In Steven Covey's book *The Seven Habits of Highly Effective People*,[2] his fifth principle is "Seek first to understand, then to be understood." In other words, before jumping in and explaining one's opinion or stance on an issue, he or she should hear the other person's point of view. He or she should hear it well enough to be able to repeat it back in a way that the other says is exactly what was meant. Then both parties can express their ideas. Covey would suggest that the other person then repeat what he or she thought was said, to the listener's satisfaction. Once this is done, a much richer and more effective communication will occur.

VERBAL COMMUNICATION

How people communicate with their voice can tell a lot about them. Certainly, vocabulary, ability to speak in grammatically correct English, and minimization of slang or "empty" words (eg, "um," "like") are important when performing in a professional capacity. The manner in which words are spoken can contradict or reinforce the meaning apparent in those words. These vocal messages include tone, pitch, emphasis, inflection, volume, vocabulary, pronunciation, dialect, and fluency. Studies have shown these factors to be as much as five times more potent than the actual words uttered.[3]

Paying attention to verbal communication is important because what is said and how it is said determines how one is perceived and understood. Expressing oneself well will result in better outcomes. The manner of presenting what needs to be said can create credibility.

Clarity is a skill that must be learned and practiced. It has several components:

1. *Use language that is appropriate to the listener and situation.* Knowing the terms of the profession is vital when communicating with other athletic trainers and related professionals. It is constructive to use the jargon of the profession in these situations for clarity and succinctness. However, one needs to "code-switch" when talking with athletes, parents, and administrators who do not know medical terms. It is not usually constructive to give explanations using terms with which others are unfamiliar. Adopt a lexicon of ways to say the same thing, but at different listeners' levels of understanding.
2. *Nonverbal messages must be consistent with verbal messages.*
3. *Be organized in expression—know what to say and say it a logical way.*
4. *Speak distinctly and audibly—speak up, articulate well, and say words properly.*
5. *Encourage feedback.*

Sometimes the receiver hears something very different than what the speaker intended to communicate. To combat this, ask the other person to paraphrase what has been said. This is very effective in determining, for example, if an athlete has understood clearly the directions he or she has been given for caring for an injury. In other situations—for example, when chairing a committee—present yourself as being receptive to questions and confrontations. Feedback, although sometimes difficult to take, helps us know if we are on target and assists us in personal and professional growth.

Nonverbal Communication

Knapp[4] reports that Ray Birdwhistell, generally considered a noted authority on nonverbal behavior, estimates the average person speaks words only 10 to 11 minutes daily, with a typical sentence taking approximately 2.5 seconds. He says that in normal two-person conversation, the verbal components carry less than 35% of the social meaning, with more than 65% of the social meaning carried by nonverbal activity.

Nonverbal communication is much more telling than any other form of communication. Studies show that no matter what is said, people will interpret the meaning by nonverbal communication. Deep and Sussman[2] sum up the power of this mode of communication (Table 6-2).

Knapp[4] says that the face is the primary site for communication of emotion, interpersonal attitudes, and nonverbal feedback in response to others. He says that next to human speech it is the primary source of information. Other body language is also very telling, including gestures (for example, these may connote anger, warmth, or disgust), brow movement (for example, furrowed—questioning or anger; raised—questioning or disbelief), and head movement (nodding—approval or disapproval; lowered—discouraged or thinking).

Another important nonverbal communication skill is active listening. To be an effective listener requires attending to the person speaking and consciously performing several response behaviors. First, be sure to react to the message, not the person. Pay attention to the person's nonverbal behaviors to see if they are congruent with the message. Appreciate the speaker's emotion behind the words and the nonverbal behaviors more than the literal meaning of the words. Try to imagine yourself in the other person's position to gain an appreciation of his or her point of view. Let your own body language indicate interest and engagement (lean forward, do not cross the arms, employ good eye contact, do not be distracted by ideas or physical surroundings). Respond to the other person's main ideas with empathy and give feedback. If important facts are being stated, write them down so you do not forget—this also shows the speaker that what he or she is saying has some value to you. Be sure to maintain as much eye contact as possible to stay engaged with the speaker.

INTERPERSONAL SKILLS

Superior clinical and cognitive skills are of no use in the athletic training profession if the athletic trainer has not developed effective interpersonal skills. It is not uncommon to have to communicate ideas, requests, or decisions to administrators, athletes, coaches, parents, physicians, colleagues, or businesses on a daily basis. How we respond to being supervised or being a supervisor, how we listen to clients or parents, how we react to controversy, how we accept responsibility, how we answer the telephone, how we write memos, and how we teach others all demand diplomacy, sensitivity, tact, consistency, honesty, and perception. It is

Table 6-2

WAYS WE SEND MESSAGES WITHOUT WORDS

- Eyes—These are the most communicative part of the body. The eyes are where to look to see if someone is happy, sad, interested, intense, surprised, lying, sick, or a dozen other conditions. The sender has very little control over what the eyes say. They are often referred to as "the windows of the soul."

- Face—The mouth can scowl, grimace, pout, smile, or communicate pompousness. Flushed cheeks may reveal discomfort, embarrassment, or a lack of physical stamina. A raised eyebrow can quiet a child.

- Hair—Some people make judgments of others based on the color of their hair, as well as whether the color appears to be natural. The amount of hair a man has remaining on his head may speak to some, as may whether, and how well, a mustache or beard is maintained. Hairstyle is often viewed as an indicator of a person's character, religious beliefs, or socioeconomic status. Graying hair sometimes elicits erroneous assumptions about abilities.

- Body—Our society draws profound inferences (and not always consistent ones) about people according to whether they are tall, short, fat, or thin.

- Posture—Leaning, kneeling, slouching, slumping, or standing erect all create distinct images in the minds of others.

- Gestures—Hand movements either reinforce or contradict what is said, and can even serve as effective substitutes for words.

- Clothing—Books have been written about the "shouting" that clothes do, especially in professional settings.

- Cosmetics—Well-applied makeup can create a positive impression; sloppy cosmetics can likewise send unfavorable messages. Perfumes and colognes have the same power.

- Accessories—Some draw inferences about people according to the things they carry around with them: eg, the looks of purses or wallets, the presence or absence of briefcases and the quality of same, the particular newspapers tucked under their arms, whether they are holding umbrellas.

- Touch—Despite recently developed taboos on touch in the workplace, service workers, especially in the health professions, are being taught how to use touch to improve their rapport with clients. The most important touch message is the handshake, which also tells a lot about the other person.

- Behavior—In Ecclesiastes it is said that "Words show the wit of man, but actions his meaning." People constantly observe behavior and from it glean what they consider to be the truth behind spoken words.

- Space—*Physical* space messages exist in the places people live and work. For example, what does your office say about you? Does its size and location speak to your importance in the company? Is the desk messy? Where are the side chairs located? Are family pictures present? What do the furniture, books, and graffiti say about their owner? *Personal* space is the distance maintained between yourself and others when in conversation, and whether you violate what they establish as their personal space.

- Place—Do you choose locations for your conversations that will reinforce, and not detract from, the meaning you want the listener to receive? Also, be aware that meeting "on your turf" (e.g., your office) versus another's office or a neutral space will change the dynamics of comfort level of the participants. A neutral place is often most comfortable for everyone.

- Time—What does your use of time say to others? Do you keep people waiting and get to meetings late? Do you often fail to deliver by agreed-upon deadlines?

Adapted from Deep and Sussman.²

important to develop the ability to share knowledge and ideas with others if one is to develop into an effective professional.

Understanding differences can make people much more effective in dealing with daily interpersonal interaction. C.G. Jung's theory of psychological types was used by Myers and Briggs to create the Myers-Briggs Type Indicator® (MBTI®) assessment instrument. This instrument is used widely in industry, sports, and psychology to help determine people's preferences in how they take in and process information.

Other inventories, such as Kolb's Learning Style, are also available to help discern learning style preferences. For illustrative purposes, the MBTI® instrument will be used as an example of how people differ in processing information. The theory of MBTI assessment is that seemingly chance variation in human behavior is not by chance at all; it is the logical result of a few basic differences in how we function mentally.[5]

These basic differences concern the way people *prefer* to use their minds; specifically, the way they perceive and the way they make judgments. *Perceiving* is here understood to include the processes of becoming aware of things, people, occurrences, and ideas. *Judging* includes the processes of coming to conclusions about what has been perceived. Together, perception and judgment, which make up a large portion of people's total mental activity, govern much of their outer behavior, because perception—by definition—determines what people see in a situation, and their judgment determines what they decide to do about it. Thus, it is reasonable that basic differences in perception or judgment should result in corresponding differences in behavior.[5]

The MBTI® instrument provides data on four sets of preferences. These preferences are referred to as people's "type." Each set of preferences is described below followed by preferences in work settings, modified from *Introduction to Type*.[6]

Extraversion Versus Introversion

This preference relates to how people take in the world around them. Extraverts have an antenna out at all times and notice everything around them. They are energized when surrounded by people and things. They are "on-the-fly" thinkers and often seem to have the motto "ready, fire, aim." They express themselves freely and easily. They prefer to have many people around them in order to recharge their batteries and get energized for more activity. Time spent alone drains their energy.

Introverts are reflective and prefer to spend a lot of time with their inner world of ideas, concepts, and abstractions. They are energized by quiet times alone. They concentrate with reflection and seem to have the motto "Ready, aim, fire" with a well-thought plan. They prefer to go to their office, shut the door, and spend time alone to recharge their batteries and get energized for more activity. Large groups drain their energy.

COMMUNICATING AND WORKING WITH EXTROVERTS

Extraverts like variety and action, enjoy interacting with people, and develop their ideas through discussion. They learn new tasks by talking and doing and are interested in how other people do their work.

COMMUNICATING AND WORKING WITH INTROVERTS

Introverts like quiet for concentration and enjoy focusing on a project or task. They develop their ideas internally and enjoy working alone with no interruptions. They learn new tasks by reading and reflecting.

This demonstration of how people prefer to take in the world around them and their resultant characteristics—introversion versus extraversion—is illustrative of the utility of knowledge of people's preferences to help understand others' actions and reactions. This is especially true when interacting with a person with a different preference from your own. Understanding and appreciating the differences will make you respond and act in different, more productive ways.

Sensing Versus Intuition

The second set of preferences deals with how information is handled.

Sensing individuals rely heavily on their five senses to gather and make sense of information. They want and trust facts and details. Intuitive individuals operate using a sixth sense, or intuition. They look for patterns and relationships and trust their "hunches." They look for the big picture versus facts.

COMMUNICATING AND WORKING WITH SENSING TYPES

Sensing individuals focus on immediate issues. They provide a realistic and practical perspective and build to conclusions by collecting facts. They like to perfect standard ways to do things by fine tuning and draw on their own and others' expertise.

COMMUNICATING AND WORKING WITH INTUITIVE TYPES

Intuitive individuals follow their inspirations and like to solve new, complex problems. They provide connections and meanings, start with the big picture and fill in the facts, and prefer change and new ways of doing things.

Thinking Versus Feeling

This preference deals with how people make decisions.

Thinking individuals prefer to make decisions based on impersonal logic and analysis—decisions made from the head. They value fairness and using objective criteria. Feeling individuals prefer to make decisions based on human values. They value harmony. Decisions are made from the heart.

COMMUNICATING AND WORKING WITH THINKING TYPES

People with the thinking preference focus on tasks, use logical analysis to understand and make decisions, apply principles consistently, and want mutual respect and fairness among colleagues. They are firm-minded and can give criticism when appropriate.

COMMUNICATING AND WORKING WITH FEELING TYPES

The person with a feeling preference focuses on people's interactions, uses values to understand and decide, applies values consistently, and wants harmony and support among colleagues. He or she is empathetic and prefers to accommodate and reach consensus.

Judging Versus Perceptive

This preference deals with lifestyle.

Judging types like to postpone action and seek more data. They are organized, decisive, and self-regulated. They are very task-oriented and pay attention to details. Deadlines are sacred. They like to have "to-do" lists. Perceptive types are curious, adaptable, and spontaneous. They begin many tasks at once and often find it difficult to complete any of them. They often do not complete tasks until the very last minute or want to stretch deadlines in case new information might arise. They rarely have "to-do" lists.

COMMUNICATING AND WORKING WITH JUDGING TYPES

Judging individuals want to plan their work and follow the plan, like to get things settled and finished, and feel supported by structure and schedules. They focus on timely completion of a project and reach closure by deciding quickly.

COMMUNICATING AND WORKING WITH PERCEPTIVE TYPES

Perceiving individuals want to have flexibility in their work, like to be spontaneous, and feel restricted by structure and schedules. They focus on enjoying the process and leave situations open as long as possible.

The combinations of preferences make individuals even more interesting to understand. For example, a sensing preference combined with perception tends to always see humor in things and is often the "class clown."

This chapter is not intended to give a complete understanding of MBTI® assessment, but to point out that all people have preferences in how they operate on a daily basis. These differences should be embraced and seen as an opportunity for even greater solutions to problems. However, if a person fails to recognize that a colleague prefers to function with a style opposite his or her own, he or she is likely to become frustrated and angry instead of understanding and tolerant. For example, if one prefers extroversion and judging (prefers to be with people and is very task oriented) and his or her colleague is introverted and perceptive (prefers to work alone and tends to leave tasks to complete until the last minute), there is tremendous potential for conflict. If one understands that a colleague is energized by being alone and will meet the deadline on exactly the due date, not 2 weeks in advance, for example, the tension is removed and communication remains good.

For those interested in taking the MBTI® assessment (Form G or Form M), it is available at many universities' counseling centers. It is a very reliable method of assessing learning style. It is used by many corporations to help managers learn how to communicate better, by most US Olympic teams to assist coaches in knowing how to motivate individual athletes, and in many organizations to assist in creating effective teams and committees. If all the same "types" are on a committee, the end result will be limited. If a heterogeneous committee is created, the processing of information will be more elaborate and the end result will be much richer. It should be noted that whatever a person's preferred type, he or she is quite capable of operating in the manner of the opposite type, just not as comfortably.

ETHNICITY AND CULTURAL DIFFERENCES

Awareness and knowledge of cultural differences and ethnic customs is essential in the global society in which we live. The United States is known as a melting pot for all cultures and Canada is known as a cultural mosaic. These two different ways of viewing the increasing population of non-Caucasians is in itself a study: in the United States, cultures attempt to become "Americanized"; in Canada, cultures are encouraged to celebrate their differences. Regardless of which North American country one comes from, ethnic population numbers are increasing. Certain areas of the country (especially cities) tend to attract larger percentages of ethnic groups. Regardless of where one works, he or she has a professional responsibility to be sensitive to cultural differences and to learn how to communicate with athletes/clients in an acceptable, nonoffensive manner.

Many athletic trainers have opportunities to work at competitions both at home and abroad. Those pursuing a teaching career will have foreign students in their classes and programs. Knowing a few do's and don'ts of behavior can help prevent embarrassing or offending situations.

A handshake is the universal greeting in most parts of the world, but it is important to check this out if one knows ahead of time that he or she will be working with or visiting someone from a particular country. For example, in Nepal and Sri Lanka, the customary greeting is to place the palms of the hands together under the chin (fingers pointing upward) and slightly bow the head. In some countries, such as South Korea and Zambia, a handshake is acceptable, and often the right forearm is supported with the left hand to show respect to the person with whom one is shaking hands.

In some cultures it is considered rude to touch another person (other than the handshake greeting). Many cultures consider finger pointing rude. People from countries with a Buddhist background consider the head the most important part of the body and no one touches another person's head (not even a child's). Many Asian cultures think it is extremely rude to yawn or use a toothpick without covering one's mouth.

In some Eastern cultures, people avoid sitting or standing on a level more elevated than that of an older person or a person highly respected in society (eg, a teacher, religious leader, or parent). It is often impolite to point one's feet toward a person, and raising the voice is a sign of bad personality.

Students (and employees) from Asian countries are often misunderstood because of the tremendous respect they have for teachers/superiors. They do not feel comfortable asking questions in class or discussing topics because, to them, this is a sign of disrespect toward the teacher/superior. Their culture teaches honor and loyalty to teachers, religious leaders, and people in authority. The people are brought up with unquestioning faith that what these respected people say must be true and that it would be unheard of to question them or debate an issue. Questioning would be considered a form of insubordination.

The way people talk, write, read, and listen is often specific to their own culture. The way they present themselves (eye contact, tone of voice, topics, attitudes) to others is influenced by the beliefs and customs of the culture in which they grew up.[7]

It would behoove athletic trainers to research the customs of any foreign-born athlete/colleague with whom they will be working or any country that may be visited as an athletic trainer. The local bookstore likely will have travel books available (eg, Fodor's or Lonely Planet) for further information about the customs of specific cultures. Another good reference is "Culturegrams: The Nations Around Us," developed by David M. Kennedy, Center for International Studies at Brigham Young University. These are available at most university libraries and through Garrett Park Press, Garrett Park, MD. The Internet is another way to access cultural information. There is no excuse for offending anyone from a culturally different background. Diversity is sought out in today's workplace and accessing information to be educated in the area of cultural differences is easier today than at any time in history. When working with a foreign team (in the United States or abroad), it is necessary to become sensitive to the culture.

SUMMARY

Effective communication is a key to success in the workplace as well as one's personal life. Communication involves many arenas (oral, written, computer-generated, and nonverbal). What one does (body actions) speaks much louder than what one says. If congruence between the verbal and nonverbal message conveyed is lacking, the speaker will come across as inauthentic and risk losing the confidence of the patient or colleague.

Understanding learning styles (one's own and others') is invaluable in understanding the differences among people. This understanding helps one to relate more effectively with others. Cultural and ethnic differences must also be recognized and appreciated in order to respond effectively to our rapidly diversifying society.

REFERENCES

1. National Athletic Trainers' Association. *Athletic Training Educational Competencies.* Dallas, TX: National Athletic Trainers' Association; 1999.

2. Covey SR. *The Seven Habits of Highly Effective People.* New York, NY: Simon & Schuster; 1989.

3. Deep S, Sussman L. *The Manager's Book of Lists.* Glenshaw, PA: S.D.D. Publishers; 1988.

4. Knapp ML. *Essentials of Nonverbal Communication.* New York, NY: Holt, Rinehart, & Winston; 1980.

5. Myers IB, Myers PB. *Gifts Differing: Understanding Personality Type.* Palo Alto, CA: Consulting Psychologists Press; 1993.

6. Myers IB. *Introduction to Type.* 6th ed. Palo Alto, CA: Consulting Psychologists Press; 1998.

7. Thomas CT, Correa VI, Morsink CV. *Interactive Teaming.* Englewood, NJ: Prentice-Hall; 1995.

Chapter Seven

Professional Behavior

"We are what we repeatedly do—excellence then is not an act, but a habit."
Aristotle

OBJECTIVES

On completion of this chapter, the student will be able to accomplish the following:

- Explain why developing a personal relationship with a client is discouraged
- Explain the components of portraying a professional image and why this is important in athletic training
- Explain and give examples of how actions speak louder than words
- Discuss the importance of maintaining a positive professional attitude

This chapter is relevant to several affective competencies. Under Health Care Administration in the *Athletic Training Educational Competencies*[1] (see Appendix A):

- Recognizes and accepts the importance of good public relations with the media (radio, TV, press), the general public, other medical and allied health care personnel, and legislators

Under Professional Development and Responsibilities:

- Defends the responsibility to interpret and promote athletic training as a professional discipline among allied health professional groups and the general public

- Accepts the responsibility to enhance the professional growth of athletic training students, colleagues, and peers through a continual sharing of knowledge, skills, values, and professional recognition

Under Psychosocial Intervention and Referral:

- Accepts the need for appropriate interpersonal relationships among all of the parties involved with athletes and others involved in physical activity

The old cliché "actions speak louder than words" is very true. It is not words but actions that reveal true character and leave a lasting impression. During this time of uncertainty among all health care providers, athletic trainers cannot afford to neglect the importance of portraying our profession and ourselves in an accurate and favorable light. One way to do that is to revisit proper etiquette for the professional settings in which athletic trainers may find themselves.

ATTITUDE

It is not what happens but how one reacts to it that matters. The only thing over which one really has control is attitude. When faced with a difficult or seemingly insurmountable situation, there are two choices: 1) to wallow in it with self-pity; or 2) to acknowledge it, rise above it, and get on with the day to day work of our lives. Certainly, it is important to reflect on events, positive and negative, that affect us in order to determine objectively how to make things better if ever in a similar circumstance. Beyond that, however, one must move on, learn from any failures, and continue with the rest of his or her life.

No matter how well-intentioned a person is, when one is not paying attention it is very easy to get caught up in negativism. It is very easy to complain and see negative things, especially if everyone around seems to be complaining. Regardless of how bad a situation may seem, however, there is always some positive aspect that can be found.

Attitudes are often formed and influenced by the people with whom one associates. During the university and early professional years, select friends well. Be sure they have moral and ethical codes similar to your own. Remember that, just as you are mentored and influenced by certain people, you are role modeling to someone all the time. It may be a younger student, an athlete, or a high school student watching from the stands. No one really knows how his or her actions and reactions may be affecting an observer. Be sure professional actions and attitudes are representing you and the profession well.

Proper Etiquette

In the clinical setting, how one greets and refers to patients and other health care personnel says a lot about him or her and the perception others have about athletic trainers. One can do much to enhance this perception. These important interactions may be face-to-face or via the telephone or Internet.

In an article about the importance of how names are used in the nursing profession,[2] the author contends that "what may seem to be a minor aspect of the health care encounter actually reflects—and perpetuates—nurses' problems with identity and status. You know the script: he's Dr. Davis, and you're just plain Judy."

The article goes on to say that using a full name represents what makes one an individual, distinguishing one from colleagues. Without exception, the author wrote, the physicians interviewed said they would not tolerate being called by their first name if professional equals were being addressed as "Mr.," "Ms.," or "Dr."

At this transitional time in health care, perhaps it would be appropriate for athletic trainers to reflect upon whether they are being treated as equals with other professionals. As you enter a first job, or a new job, it is worth considering introducing yourself using both your first and last names.

A good rule to follow if unsure of a patient's preference is to call him or her Mr. or Ms. and use the last name. This is especially true of patients older than you. Often he or she will ask to be addressed by first name, but if this does not occur, continuing to address the patient as Mr. or Ms. would be in order.

Sometimes daily routines become so ritualistic that they are performed without awareness or while one is preoccupied with other things. Answering the telephone is one of these daily routines. As in all communication, the listener forms many opinions about the speaker, and judging athletic trainers by telephone mannerisms is no exception. If one is disgruntled or in the middle of a controversy and answers with a downcast, resentful, or angry attitude, the mood will manifest itself in the voice and send a less than desirable message to the caller. Unless caller identification is on the telephone, one may end up portraying him- or herself in an unfavorable and unprofessional way to someone he or she would never want to speak to in this way (eg, a boss, a respected colleague, someone from the National Athletic Trainers' Association). The truth is, no matter who is on the receiving end, one's manner of answering the telephone should always be professional. Voices and attitudes can be controlled. True professionals can always rise above small annoyances as well as significant happenings, and consistently portray themselves in a manner that honors the athletic training profession.

Similarly, the message one leaves on both the office and home voice message system tells the caller a lot about the person being called. A student athletic trainer should be sure the message on his or her apartment/residence hall telephone portrays him or her in a favorable way. Faculty, staff, athletes, and potential employers may call on occasion. Whereas unconventional, humorous messages may be entertaining for a brief moment to a peer, it could mean the difference between getting an interview or opportunity and not being considered. Even as you enter the workforce and get your first job, never underestimate who might call you at home and what impression may be given by the voice message. Poor discretion will probably not cause you to lose your job, but it may cause the caller to question your maturity and professional level.

The increasing possibilities of expressing ourselves via the Internet and through conference calls, teleconferencing, and interactive television require attention to additional messages we send about ourselves and the profession. E-mail and chatboxes are wonderful opportunities for exchanges of ideas and information. As in any written communication, be sure to check messages you are sending for spelling and grammar. It is very easy to respond/react quickly to an e-mail and just send the reply without reviewing it, believing that as long as the receiver gets the main message, the typographical errors are not that critical. The problem with this rationale is twofold: 1) as a professional, there is never a good excuse to send anything in writing that is not checked and corrected for spelling and grammar; and 2) many times messages are printed and the errors then become more glaring—especially when the message is shared with others. Again, communication and attention to detail say a lot about a person and his or her profession.

Be aware that information shared in chatbox dialogue may or may not be accurate, even if the chatbox is visited only by athletic trainers. Sometimes one person's well-intentioned but uninformed stance creates unnecessary concern or incorrect assumptions. If a professional issue of great concern to you is being discussed, be sure to go directly to a source who will know all the facts (often your district director or state president) before making a judgment.

Conference calls are often used to conduct interviews or to hold meetings. The person arranging the conference call should inform you of the protocol (what to expect when the call comes in terms of waiting for all parties to get on the line as well as the procedure for progressing through the meeting). Obviously only one person can speak at a time. If it is an interview, often the people conducting the interview are at one site and the interviewee at another. The interviewers usually introduce themselves individually and, if appropriate, indicate their title or position as it relates to the call. If it is a meeting where the participants are at multiple sites, after all participants are connected, the facilitator usually does a roll call to be sure that everyone can hear everyone else. Depending on the nature of the meeting, you may be called upon to give your input or, if you have an opinion, you begin speaking by giving your name so that everyone else knows who is speaking.

Teleconferencing involves sitting at a remote site (ie, a site that is away from the site where the presentation is actually being delivered) while the presentation is downlinked to a television or screen. There are times throughout the presentation when one can call in questions to the presenters. The facilitator at your site will either request that you write your question down and he or she will call it in at the designated time or ask you to call the question in yourself. Often you are not identified by name, but by the location of your site.

Interactive television is an effective way to hold meetings or conduct classes. Two or more sites are connected and as you sit in a room at one site with a camera on you and others at that site, colleagues at the other sites are watching you in real time (you also are seeing them on a television screen in your room). Your nonverbal messages and activity during this type of meeting are visible to all participants and obviously a professional demeanor is called for. Attire is important and wearing a baseball cap or chewing gum, for example, would be inappropriate.

Thank-you notes or letters are also very important. Whether the purpose is to express gratitude to a colleague for assisting you, to a superior who played a role in getting you funding, or to a parent or athlete who may have given you a gift, a simple, sincerely sent note can speak volumes about you and ultimately reflect on the profession. Although the Internet is easy and quick to access to send a thank-you message, the extra time and effort put into sending a card or note in the mail may send a more meaningful message. Certainly a message via Internet is acceptable and better than nothing at all.

One area many do not consider is proper eating etiquette. Many university career centers now offer workshops on the correct way to eat a seven-course meal (which utensils to use when, how to eat various foods properly, and other appropriate table manners). This is important to know in case you are taken to a fine restaurant during an interview or for a meeting with a supervisor, or you are asked to entertain a guest.

An earlier chapter discussed professional commitment and part of that is a commitment to the institution where one works. Unless you have strong philosophical differences or are compromising your values, you should show respect for your supervisors and heed their instructions and protocols. If you cannot be happy in the position and cannot respect your supervisors or colleagues, it may be time for you to consider finding a new job that better matches your values and philosophy.

PUBLIC AND PRIVATE BEHAVIOR

Whenever you are in a public forum, someone is watching your behavior. Whether you are a student athletic trainer, newly certified and in your first job, or an experienced athletic trainer, this will not change. Not only does your behavior reflect your workplace; it has a profound effect on perceptions of the athletic training profession. This is particularly true when an observer is not familiar with what athletic trainers do and assumes that what you present (whether by appearance, words, or action) is representative of all athletic trainers and the profession.

What people do in their private lives is entirely their business, although there are some ethical considerations if that private behavior involves relationships with patients. Much has been written by many of the health care professions cautioning professionals to avoid personal, especially sexual, relationships with patients. If a psychologist or social worker develops a personal relationship with a client, he or she is at risk of losing his or her license. The reason for the caution is because of the potential for conflict of interest and, more importantly, the potential for the patient to be taken advantage of or for abuse of authority in this position. This is why many curriculum programs have a policy that does not permit student athletic trainers to date athletes who are on the team to which they are assigned. Even the most inconspicuous, well-thought-out relationship can end up causing conflicts that place the athletic trainer in a compromising position.

"The protective nature of the caregiver's relationship with a patient is shattered when a sexual involvement develops, regardless of who initiated it. Because of the nature of our obligations to the patient and the essential inequality of our interactions, sexual relationships are always wrong. It is the clear responsibility of the caregiver to recognize when the potential for such an involvement exists and take action to avoid it."[3]

Whereas no one has the right to say who you can date and not date, if an attraction exists, it is best to inform your supervisor (curriculum director) of the conflict and request to be assigned to a different sport.

SELF-DISCLOSURE

Self-disclosure means talking to patients about personal aspects of your life and expressing your feelings about issues in your life. Self-disclosure rarely has a place in the athletic trainer–patient relationship.

A certain amount of self-disclosure can be part of an effective professional/client relationship, but thought and discretion must be used. The following scenario from the medical field can serve as an example of too much self-disclosure[3]:

"Consider the scenario of a physician who discloses details of his or her weekend activities to a patient in general conversation. When the doctor reveals a penchant for wine and cigarettes, credibility with this patient, and any others to whom this patient may talk, is seriously undermined. As a result, the doctor's attempt to persuade this patient, who is suffering from heart disease, that he ought to quit smoking and decrease his alcohol intake may be less successful."

It does not take much imagination to see how similar indiscreet behavior in the athletic trainer/athlete role could diminish the effectiveness of the relationship. Further, other athletes or your coworkers may assume that, because of your extracurricular activities, you may be less reliable for some tasks than are other athletic trainers.

PROFESSIONAL MANNERS

Graciousness and courtesy are two ingredients that too often are in short supply in our hectic, fast-paced, pressure-filled workplaces. Patients and other constituents can sense the mood in the office they are visiting. "Patients can sense when their caregivers have respect for each other and feel assured that they, too, will be treated with dignity."[3]

Breaches in good manners are far too commonplace in today's society and can carry over into the athletic training environment if we are not careful in how we treat each other. We have the right to expect that colleagues and the clients with whom we work will be polite. Having a busy schedule, being a nationally recognized figure, or having a bad day do not make one exempt from the rules of civility and good manners.

PROFESSIONAL IMAGE

First impressions are extremely important and the image any athletic trainer portrays sends a powerful statement about athletic trainers in general. In the mid-1980s, the National Athletic Trainers' Association (NATA) invited a news anchor from a national network to present a session on professional image and to give her impression on the image of athletic trainers. Her remarks were profound and on target. She first talked about the fact that as a woman and a national TV personality, she had to do much more than her male counterparts to "look good" (in terms of, for example, attire, hair style, and makeup) in front of the cameras. If she did not portray a very professional, conservative look, the viewers would not perceive her as the best and would choose other stations to watch. This ultimately could cost her a job. Her point was that whether we like it or not, we are judged by the way we look. An initial impression is often a lasting one. As for women in the profession, although the NATA membership is equally represented by men and women, there are still places women will work that are male dominated, and women may need to work twice as hard to be accepted and respected. Everything an athletic trainer can do within the bounds of professionalism and his or her own ethical standards to earn the respect of others should be done. Attire may be one area that should be targeted (Figure 7-1).

The TV anchor's response to the question of athletic trainers' image was very revealing. She looked out over the audience members—a few of whom were

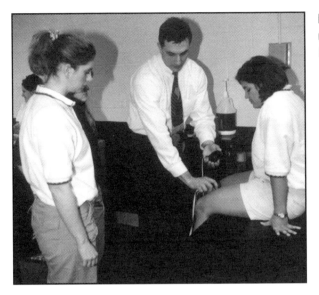

Figure 7-1. Athletic trainers must role model a professional image. Photograph by John Papa.

dressed in business clothes or business casual, but many of whom were wearing shorts, golf or tee shirts, and running shoes—and said that she would not have known it was a professional meeting by looking at the members' attire. She cautioned that any other health profession's national meeting would be characterized by professional attire, and never with shorts, tee shirts, and sandals. She went on to say that how we portray ourselves has a big impact on how we are perceived. Some athletic trainers were offended at her comments and others were in agreement and applauded the fact that someone had the courage to address this issue. Since that time, and especially in recent years, the NATA administration has gone so far as to mention proper attire in convention registration materials.

When attending any official function as an athletic trainer (whether at the work site, in the community, or at conventions), choice of attire reflects respect for the profession and the colleagues with whom one will interact. Unless prior arrangements have been agreed upon (eg, a dress down day at a place of employment or an agreement that shorts or warm-ups will be acceptable for a particular casual meeting), dress professionally. We all need to take responsibility for the profession's image.

Every day we are submerged in a world of choices. We make many choices subconsciously throughout any given day. For example, our morning routine as we get out of bed, the location of the seat when we sit in class, and the way we greet people are all choices. We could, if we thought about it, change any of the ways we do these things. They are so automatic and routine that, unless something breaks the pattern (eg, the power goes out in the morning just as you are getting up or you enter a classroom and someone has changed the seating arrangement from rows of desks to a large circle), we do not even realize that there is a choice.

It is also true that unless we realize that there are professional choices facing us daily, we run the risk of unconsciously portraying an image of which we are totally unaware. The most obvious example is our attitude. As Abraham Lincoln stated, "You're about as happy as you make up your mind to be."

CONSCIENTIOUSNESS

Webster's[4] defines conscientiousness as:

1. Scrupulous
2. Done according to one's moral sense of right and wrong

Conscientiousness goes beyond simply knowing and abiding by the profession's code of ethics. It reflects the individual's code of ethics and value system. Health professions require a high level of conscientiousness. Athletic training professionals may require even more because of the decisions to be made regarding athletes' return to play. Scenarios occur in which a physician clears an athlete to play in a game, but the athlete cannot meet functional test criteria. In situations like this, the athletic trainer needs to be able to make a decision, accept the consequences, and most importantly, be able to live with his or her conscience. Personal responsibility, accountability, and personal ethics/values coupled with honesty, reliability, and follow-through demonstrate conscientiousness.

SUMMARY

Professional behavior is difficult to define and even harder to measure. It is unquestionably one of the most important, although underemphasized, aspects of professional preparation. Our actions speak volumes about who we are and portray the profession (whether in a favorable or unfavorable light) to the public. Our responsibility to promote athletic training as a professional discipline among other professional groups and the general public as well as to enhance the professional growth of colleagues and peers requires us to be conscious and aware of our daily patterns that define professional behavior to those around us. Each of us plays a major role in continually improving and sustaining athletic training's professional image.

REFERENCES

1. National Athletic Trainers' Association. *Athletic Training Educational Competencies.* Dallas, TX: National Athletic Trainers' Association; 1999.

2. Gordon S, Grady M. What's in a name? *Am J Nurs.* 1995;95:31–33.

3. Parsons HP, Parsons AH. *Health Care Ethics.* Middletown, OH: Wall & Emerson; 1992.

4. Neufeldt V, ed. *Webster's New Word Dictionary of American English.* New York, NY: Simon & Schuster; 1988.

Chapter Eight

Employer/Employee Roles and Responsibilities

"Every calling is great when greatly pursued."
Oliver Wendell Holmes

OBJECTIVES

On completion of this chapter, the student will be able to accomplish the following:

- Differentiate between jobs and careers and apply the concepts to create their own career path
- Describe the essential skills needed to survive and thrive in a global society
- Explain how to prepare for a job interview
- Explain how to go about establishing oneself in a new work environment

This chapter is relevant to the following affective competency from Professional Development and Responsibilities of the *Athletic Training Educational Competencies*[1] (see Appendix A):

- Accepts the professional, historical, ethical, and organizational structures that define the proper roles and responsibilities of the certified athletic trainer in providing health care to athletes and others involved in physical activity

Careers/Global Opportunities

Unlike past generations, the current cohort entering the workforce can anticipate changing jobs or careers 8 to 12 times before they retire. This is quite different from the days when employees would enter a career after graduation and often remain with the same job for 30 to 40 years until retirement. The job security this afforded is all but lost in the current atmosphere of downsizing, mergers, and increased global opportunity. Despite the knowledge that entering professionals will change jobs multiple times throughout their working years, it is important to plan a career and look at career ladders versus just striving to get the first job. A corollary to this is that a job should be treated as a career stepping stone versus 8:00 AM to 5:00 PM work. There is much more to a career than a paycheck. It is critically important to see and identify avenues for advancement and professional growth. Being purposefully aware, or failing to be aware, of career development is entirely one's own responsibility. Networking and discussions with mentors help make one aware of options, obstacles, and opportunities.

It should be noted that for new professionals, the career path has a pyramid appearance, with fewer positions available the further up it they climb.[2] That is, there are many more entry-level jobs than head athletic trainer jobs, faculty jobs, or program director jobs. Similarly, there are proportionately more volunteer jobs and committee positions available at the local and state level than the regional and the national level of the National Athletic Trainers' Association (NATA). In the job setting, there is much variability depending on college, high school, clinic, industrial, or nontraditional settings.

Personal constraints such as geographic location, dual career considerations, "stop out" periods for childbirth or child rearing, the regional job market, and other considerations should be taken into account. Awareness and development of excellence in practice are necessary to succeed, advance, and thrive in today's competitive workplace.

The chances of having an opportunity to gain experience or work in a foreign country are very real. With technology making international connections in less than a second and with increasing business and healthcare mergers and global expansions, it would be worthwhile to take advantage of any opportunity that would allow one to experience internationalism. Cross-cultural competence would open doors for new employees. Many universities offer classes or student exchanges in foreign countries. In a university setting, check with the Office of International Studies/Initiatives to see if any might be of interest. Foreign language study is also an asset. International athletic competitions held in one's own home-land usually need volunteer athletic trainers to assist the host site with the day-to-day running of the event. This is a good way to gain exposure to different cultures.

Prior chapters in this book have emphasized that a number of skills, attitudes, characteristics, and abilities beyond academic training are needed in order to succeed in the workplace. These are also necessary for international employment. In addition, one group of employers has suggested a list of "essential" skills necessary to succeed in an international environment[3]:

- Ability to learn
- Adventurous spirit
- Creativity
- Curiosity
- Functional skills
- Good sense of humor
- Initiative
- Language skills
- Strong interpersonal skills
- Sensitivity, adaptability, and flexibility
- Tenacity
- Willingness to take risks

It also follows that an international experience reflects that one is a risk-taker, is willing to take initiative, is not afraid of challenge or change, has tenacity, is adventuresome, and is willing and able to learn new things. This is a profound statement on a résumé and may cause one application to rise to the top among other candidates. Other experiences and skills that can help make a résumé stronger were suggested in Chapter 3.

PROFESSIONAL RÉSUMÉS

Information on the skill of creating an effective résumé is readily available through campus career centers and the NATA web page (www.nata.org – scroll to Placement Vacancy and click on Athletic Training Employment Issues Handbook & Guide). Résumés should reflect significant accomplishments in as clear and precise a manner as possible. They should be accompanied by a cover letter highlighting key strengths relative to the job description and qualities that make the applicant different. Many employers will discard résumés with typographical errors, with misspelling of their name, or that arrive in handwritten versus typed envelopes. If the advertisement indicates that an applicant should send an application to a department (eg, Personnel Department), make telephone calls to find out the name of the Personnel Director or Chairperson of the search committee so the letter can be addressed to a person.

Computers have significantly increased the possibilities for style and format of résumés. However, a few basic principles that err on the side of conservatism warrant mentioning. First, choose a font style that is readable. If the style is ornate or "busy" and causes the page to "dance," it will create difficulty for the reader. Anything less than a font size of 10 to 12 points is too small. With computer assistance much more information can be forced onto one page while maintaining readability. If the increased volume of information is not well-structured, of appropriate size, and readable, the employer will not spend extra time trying to decipher the credentials.

Use conservatively colored paper—preferably white or off-white. Most employers are turned off by neon colors and some other colors are distracting. With the advent of résumé scanners, white or off-white ensures that the scanner will read all of your information. A laser-printed original is the best to send, although a typewritten original or high-quality photocopy will suffice. Do not send a dot-matrix printed résumé or a low-quality copy.

Keep in mind that "Hundreds of large companies . . . use types of text-searching or artificial-intelligence software to track résumés. Midsize companies are also beginning to use the software as vendors start marketing cheaper web-based versions."[4] Since 1998, a rapidly growing number of employers have been wading through large volumes of applications by using computers to scan and select the best résumés before a human being ever looks at them. Scanning is being used at increasing rates in business and education. The scan is searching for key words (nouns) that are germane to the job description. Therefore, a résumé should include concrete words rather than vague concepts (eg, "organized and assigned sport coverage for three state championships" versus "responsible for assignment of sport coverage"). Describe your personal traits using key words such as "dependable", "leader", "high energy", "team player", and "skilled in time management". Be aware of key words in the job announcement and use them. Look at athletic training journals and talk to other professionals to learn other key words that employers might find attractive.

To maximize scannability, use plain or off-white paper, printed on one side only. Do not use boldface, underlining, italics, or shading (they can confuse the scanner). Do not fold your résumé—the crease is often read as a line.

Usually, but not always, the employer will tell you if the résumé will be scanned. Having two résumés is useful in today's marketplace—one for computers to scan and one for readers to read. Résumés that survive the scanner/screening process are then read by search committees.

Job Description

At the interview stage of any job, it is advisable to request a copy of the job description. Most job advertisements give highlights of the tasks expected, but the actual job description is more detailed. Be sure to read this before accepting any job. It is especially important to have your own copy of the description once you have accepted a position. This document becomes important in two ways: 1) it spells out exactly what is expected and can be used by the employee or the employer to determine if an employee is meeting the expectations of the job; 2) it is useful if the place of employment expects the employee to take on additional responsibilities not included in the original job description. Over time, depending on the magnitude and nature of additional work, the employee could show that his or her duties have increased and use this as a bargaining tool (eg, for a new computer, time off, funding for a conference, a pay raise, or a promotion).

Interviews

Career centers at all universities have tips on how to conduct oneself at an interview. Employers are looking for honest, motivated, self-confident, flexible employees with good interpersonal, communication, teamwork, analytical, and leadership skills. Be sure to research the workplace where you will be interviewing. This shows that you have initiative and are able to fact-find independently. Finding out as much about the organization as possible will help the applicant decide if the job fits his or her expectations and comfort level.

First impressions are very important—how you are dressed and how you carry yourself (relaxed and confident or rigid and timid) say a lot about you. (Be sure to go the extra mile in terms of clothing appearance—ie, send the outfit to be dry cleaned and/or properly pressed if it is wrinkled.) Michelle Compton states: "It does not matter if the company dress code is jeans and T-shirts, a dark suit or dress is the preferred professional business attire for creating a good first impression."[5]

The biggest mistakes include trying to take over the interview, not preparing, treating subordinates improperly (eg, the secretary), and misrepresenting yourself to the employer by relaying misleading information in the interview or on the résumé. Personality and mannerisms are very important, accompanied by a firm handshake, good eye contact, and asking of perceptive, in-depth questions that give substance to the process. Again, knowledge of the organization and its mission are essential before going on the interview.

When arriving for the interview, remember that to be on time is to be late. Plan for the unexpected (eg, transportation problems, traffic jams, wrong directions) and arrive at the interview site early. This allows for time to become relaxed and familiar with the surroundings and to concentrate and focus on the process. Have a prepared list of questions, written down, to ask the committee. Most search committees are impressed when they can tell by the questions that you have knowledge of their organization and their mission. Listen carefully to the questions being asked. If necessary, take a moment to reflect on the answer. Be sure the response clearly addresses the essence of the question and does not wander off onto an unrelated topic. Be prepared to answer questions that relate to professional behavior (eg, an ethical dilemma scenario is given and you are asked how you would handle it and why). Employers are interested in how workers behave with colleagues and patients and their willingness/capacity to be team players. As stated earlier in this text, personal characteristics are increasingly more important in predicting job success than are academic and clinical skills.

Finally, be yourself in an interview. No matter how much you might want a particular job, you do not want it if you have to pretend you are someone else in order to please your employer.

LETTERS OF RESIGNATION

Accepting a new job creates excitement, some anxiety, and a preoccupation with planning the personal and professional move. It is important to write a resignation letter that reflects positively on the experiences and growth you have attained at your current place of employment. Building bridges rather than burning them, even if the job was less than desirable, is important. You never know when you might cross paths with your supervisor, colleagues, or employer in the future. In fact, it is amazing how connected the world is as we move through our professional careers. If you are departing a job setting that was a negative or stressful experience, there still have been some aspects of it that allowed you to gain professional growth or awareness. Search to identify these areas so you can mention their value in your resignation letter. Write about how the new position will allow continuation of your professional or career growth.[6] Be sure to indicate how many weeks of formal notice you are providing. If you are so inclined (especially when leaving a job you liked), offer your assistance in helping the employer with the transition (eg, a plan for coverage of events, recruitment of a replacement, or informing colleagues).

CHAIN OF COMMAND

During the job interview it would be appropriate to ask what the chain of command is at the institution. You need to know to whom you report. Ask to see a flow chart—a diagram that indicates who reports to whom and shows the power structure of the organization. Chains of command are necessary and it is important to observe the "pecking order" protocol should you ever have the desire to correspond with someone above or in a parallel position with your supervisor. Any issues should always be taken to your immediate superior first. If you wish to take it further you should inform your superior of your intentions. Nothing annoys a boss more than finding out, after the fact, that he or she has been circumvented. A major function of formal structure in organizations is to ensure fairness and equity to all constituents.[2] Be aware of your rights and responsibilities if you are part of a labor union. Often the labor contract policies and procedures will specifically indicate how you should proceed.

ESTABLISHING YOURSELF

Each workplace has its own culture and unwritten as well as written customs and norms. It is important to be aware that there is a workplace culture in all jobs and that politics are always, to one degree or another, in operation. Some places of employment offer extensive orientation programs for new hires; others offer no formal introduction. It is up to you to take the initiative to learn about where you are working and to observe how things work.

A lot of information can be obtained from written policies/procedures, mission statements, and past records/documents. Study the organizational chart and know the names of key players and actors in the organization. Some of the intangible information (eg, office politics) can be learned by observing, listening, and seeking answers from individuals who have worked there for some time.

Try to not pass judgment (positive or negative) on the appropriateness of anything you observe until you are sure you have a complete picture. When seeking advice from and observing veteran workers, keep in mind that you will eventually learn which colleagues are best to go to for their expertise, which for their truthfulness, and which for communication (how to best communicate and with whom).

If it has not been explicitly stated in your job offer or description, determine the expectations of your supervisor and be sure to meet or exceed them. Some of these can be asked directly; others can be observed. For example, keeping your supervisor informed, meeting deadlines, performing well-planned work, maintaining office hours, attending special events, and following dress codes may be noted by him or her. Observe carefully what types of things are said and not said at office meetings. Again, colleagues can be helpful in providing some of this information if it has not been clearly stated.

It is also important as a citizen to get involved in the community. Community service activities help a cause, help get you networked outside the workplace, and let others see that you are well-rounded and concerned about civic issues. Even if one chooses only a single service project (eg, one can teach cardiopulmonary resuscitation classes, collect for the Cancer Society, volunteer hours at the humane society, be active in church—there is no shortage of opportunity), the people he or she meets and works with often end up being good contacts in very unpredictable ways in the future.

Another facet of establishing yourself is knowing how to get the most out of attending a conference/workshop. The American Association of Collegiate Registrars and Admissions Officers have created an uncopyrighted brochure entitled "How to 'Do' a Conference," available also on the Internet (www.aacrao.com), with some valuable tips for first-time conference-goers. Some of the on-site tips that are worth noting include:

- Know the program and audience ahead of time and decide what two or three things you want to accomplish at the conference
- Attend any "first-time conference attendees" or "newcomers" sessions/receptions
- Attend the opening session
- Attend the business meeting (if it is an open meeting), where you can learn a lot about the organization; if it is a NATA meeting, you have a

professional obligation to be there supporting and learning about key issues

- Decide ahead of time which sessions you will attend and arrive at sessions early (this ensures you a seat)
- Visit and spend time in the exhibit hall (it is a great place to network with many free materials)
- Attend any special interest group sessions that are meaningful to you; volunteer for a committee if the opportunity arises
- Read the Conference News each day for highlights, events, and cancellations

With just a bit of effort, initiative, and awareness, you can do much more than the job description requires and be well on the way to building a foundation for a productive, progressive career in athletic training.

SUMMARY

Beginning a career versus getting a job is a very exciting time for any professional. Planning a career takes time and an awareness of the many and diverse opportunities that exist for athletic trainers. Many skills and abilities, beyond clinical and academic preparation, are necessary for success and can be learned. In order to be successful in any job search, special attention must be given to the job announcement and matching the skills on one's résumé with the key requirements for the position. Thoroughly researching the organization (eg, its mission, structure, size, and location) before sending the résumé will assist in knowing and matching your strengths with the organization's needs. This information will be invaluable at the interview stage.

Be sure to have a copy of the job description and understand what each item means before accepting a job. Knowledge of the organization's chain of command is also important. It will take some time on the job to learn the culture of the organization. It is often best to be an astute observer for awhile versus trying to make radical changes in how things are done (unless that is your employer's expectation). Locate someone you can trust to go to when advice is needed.

Finally, try to get involved with committees and projects (both in your organization as well as community). This is where you will network and begin to establish yourself as a contributing member of the organization and profession.

REFERENCES

1. National Athletic Trainers' Association. *Athletic Training Educational Competencies.* Dallas, TX: National Athletic Trainers' Association; 1999.

2. Amey MI, Reesor LM. *Beginning Your Journey: A Guide for New Professionals in Student Affairs.* Washington, DC: National Association of Student Personnel Administration; 1998.

3. National Association of Colleges and Employers. Think "job skills" first—then think international career. In: *Planning Job Choices. 1999.* Bethlehem, PA: National Association of College and Employers; 1998.

4. Pollock EJ. Inhuman resources. In: *The Wall Street Journal.* New York, NY: Dow Jones; 1998.

5. Compton M. The job search jungle. *Women in Business.* 1999;51:49.

6. Yate M. *Cover Letters That Knock 'Em Dead.* Holbrook, MA: Adams Media; 1998.

Chapter Nine

Teamwork/Collaboration

*"Almost every significant breakthrough is the result of a courageous break
with traditional ways of thinking."*
Stephen R. Covey

OBJECTIVES

On completion of this chapter, the student will be able to accomplish the
following:

- Explain the challenges and opportunities created by dwindling health
  care resources
- Explain the importance and the role of teamwork in today's workplace
- Compare and contrast traditional decision-making with consensus
  decision-making
- Identify some of the considerations necessary when teams of people
  author a work

Health care costs are continuing to escalate and providers are struggling to
maintain the same quality of care with fewer dollars. Employers in government,
education, and private organizations are examining resources and ways to utilize
them maximally. Patients and clients are increasingly wiser consumers and know
they have a choice in selecting their provider. The workplace is characterized by
the impact of a rapidly changing world (in arenas such as technology, mergers, and
health care); more work is knowledge-based, and organizations are actively seeking outsourcing as a means of cost reduction. Regardless of the work environment,
athletic trainers will need to be active participants in helping employers remain

viable and plan for the future. Becoming a team player will be one of the hallmarks of health professionals. It is no accident that teamwork is identified as one of the top skills and characteristics employers are looking for in employees.[1]

This chapter has relevance to affective competencies in the *Athletic Training Educational Competencies*[2] (see Appendix A). Under Health Care Administration:

- Respects the roles and cooperation of medical personnel, administrators, and other staff members in the organization and administration of athletic training service programs

Under Professional Development and Responsibilities:

- Respects the role and responsibilities of the other health care professions

CONSTRAINED HEALTH RESOURCES

Resources include all the means, funds, and supports necessary to produce health care and athletic training care for the athletes/patients. This includes: 1) personnel (labor), such as athletic trainers, physicians, specialists, technicians, and administrators, as well as their education, skills, and training; 2) capital expenditures (facilities and equipment; 3) land (where current facilities exist and for future expansion; and 4) "entrepreneurship"—the skills, special talents, and risk-taking that the management and employees bring to the organization. All these resources are scarce and available in limited amounts at any given time.[3]

The scarcity of resources means that we need to be proactive in ensuring that all has been done to maintain or create a place for athletic training. Resources must be managed and utilized well in order to meet, prioritize, and prepare for the future. Creativity, interdependence on each other and other health professions, willingness to share common services, and collaboration/teamwork are needed.

TEAMWORK

Common sense readily allows us to realize how important it is to not only be willing to work on a team, but to do what it takes to be a team player (Table 9-1).

Table 9-1

DO WE HAVE AS MUCH SENSE AS A GOOSE?

In the fall when you see geese in a "V" formation heading south for the winter, you might be interested to know why they fly that way. Scientists have learned that as each bird flaps its wings, it creates an uplift for the bird immediately following. By flying in the "V" formation, the whole flock adds at least 71% flying range more than if each bird were on its own. Basic Truth #1: Those who share a common direction and sense of community can get where they are going more quickly and easily because they travel on the thrust of another's efforts.

Whenever a goose falls out of formation, it suddenly feels drag and air resistance from trying to go it alone. It quickly gets back into formation to take advantage of the lifting power of the bird immediately in front. Basic Truth #2: If we have as much sense as a goose, we will stay in formation with those headed the same way as we are.

When the goose gets tired, it rotates back in the wing and another flies point. Basic Truth #3: It pays to take turns on hard jobs—for people as for southbound geese.

The geese honk from behind to encourage those up front to keep their speed. Basic Truth #4: We should offer praise and encouragement to those around us—it will help us all reach our goal faster.

Finally, when a goose gets sick or is wounded by gunshot and falls out, two geese fall out of formation and follow it down to provide help and protection. They stay with it until it is either able to fly or is dead, then set out to catch up with their flock, flying on their own or with another group. Final Truth (#5): If we have the sense of a goose we will always stand by one another.

Author Unknown

Teamwork is a responsibility that we must assume and accept in today's world of health care delivery. Teamwork is a positive process that empowers individuals (Figure 9-1).

Effective teams (including committees, task forces, and project groups) do not just happen. Just because a group is called a team does not mean it will function. Participating in a meeting, voting on issues, or working in harmony (no friction) can all happen without true teamwork.[4] The value of true teamwork is that it brings diverse people with expertise in relevant areas (and with a vested interest in the outcome) together to solve a problem, create an alternative, or complete a clearly defined objective. Teamwork creates *synergy* (the strengthening and stimu-

Figure 9-1. Teamwork empowers individuals. Photograph by John Papa.

lating that occurs when two or more people collaborate to produce results greater than the sum of their parts).[4] The collective thinking of a group of people will create a better solution than will the independent thinking of one person. Some problems require one person to make decisions; eg, something that is urgent and important, such as an athlete who has stopped breathing or an office that is on fire. Someone would obviously begin artificial respiration or pull the fire alarm and evacuate the building without calling a team of people together to deliberate on how to proceed. More complex issues in terms of issues that effect the entire department or organization are better handled with representative teams (ie, representatives from each area with a vested interest in the outcome). If the organization is a sports medicine clinic considering which of its areas to outsource, representatives from all areas (eg, athletic trainers, secretaries, physical therapists, massage therapists, exercise physiologists, and nutritionists) should all be on the team. This has two effects: it ensures that all relevant facts are heard, and, most importantly, it gives all stakeholders ownership of the final result. This model is being used in business and government and increasingly in health and education organizations. It is very different from the traditional top-down model, where an administrator confers with a few managers and dictates the mandate.

Teams are important to organizations in many respects. "What makes team determination worthwhile (even though it is more difficult) is that a team multiplies the resources which can be brought to bear on a problem. Different experiences, divergent viewpoints, different specialties, the clash of ideas and opinions—these are the stuff of synergism, and none of them is present in independent determination."[4] In addition, "The hallmark of a team is that it's a group with a purpose and that it's organized to function collaboratively and interdependently so as to achieve that purpose productively."[4]

Hopefully the case has been made for the value of teamwork and it is understandable, from an administrator's point of view, why every athletic trainer will likely end up serving on teams in the workplace. The real key to the success of a team is that all participants know that teamwork does not just happen when a group of people are put together and given a task. The task or mission must be clear, with a leader/facilitator responsible for the content and structure of team meetings as well as the dynamics of the meeting to ensure that members interact effectively. Team rules that everyone can agree upon should be established (eg, meetings will start and end on time; meetings will be held on certain days in a set time frame, no "put-downs", everyone's ideas are valuable). Training is necessary for understanding effective teams and group dynamics. Minimally, the leader/facilitator should be trained.

As a new professional, take advantage of any opportunity to learn more about group process and teamwork. It is here to stay and knowing how to plan and implement with other professionals effectively will be increasingly necessary.

One of the most important components of teamwork is reaching decisions by *consensus* (versus majority vote or individual decisions). Consensus decision-making is when the team takes ownership for the decision as a united team, fully considers the facts and alternatives, and agrees on a course of action. Consensus does not always mean that there is 100% agreement that the solution is the one best solution. It does mean that all team members can agree to the benefits of the solution and, therefore, can live with or support it. Consensus decisions are most appropriate for issues that will affect everyone, are complex and require in-depth analysis by more than one individual, and require the commitment and ownership of the entire team. Consensus decisions are likely to produce quality decisions, even though the process requires more time and effort than the "business as usual" method of majority vote.[5]

TEAM PRESENTING/AUTHORING

If one is going to submit professional work for publication or for presentation at a professional meeting collaboratively, it is very important to establish a protocol for the listing of presenters/authors. This protocol needs to be discussed and understood by all participants very early in the developing stages of the project.

After it has been decided who all the contributors will be and what they will be responsible for, it should be openly and clearly decided whose name will appear first in the citation, the order of the subsequent names, and if any persons will not be listed as presenters/authors. Failure to do this important exercise can result in misunderstandings and hard feelings at the end of the project.

Making these decisions is not an exact science and that is why early discussion is essential to avoid problems later. The person doing the initiation, organization, and majority of the work is listed as the primary (first) author, and after that it is a matter of reaching consensus on who should be listed and in what order. For presentations, everyone actually presenting should be listed, and often a copresenter is unable to attend, but because of his or her contribution, he or she is still listed in the program as a presenter. In coauthoring, there are several potential criteria that could be considered. For example, did the person assist in designing the study or grant, the literature review and writing, data collection, securing subjects, providing financial support, writing the manuscript, or editing the work? Should all of these be weighted equally? How many of them would be necessary to have a name listed as an author? This process has potential for causing conflict if it is not clearly spelled out at the front end of the process.

If planning on doing any research that involves human subjects (even questionnaires), be sure to explain (in writing) the study, what you intend to do with the results, and what benefits, if any, the subjects will receive, and then obtain their written consent. They need to be assured of anonymity and confidentiality. They also need to know all persons involved in the research and full disclosure of support you are receiving. Research subjects' well-being are protected by federal regulations. Most institutions where you will be employed will have detailed human subjects procedures. You will be held responsible for knowing and abiding by these for any research you undertake.

SUMMARY

The economy, especially in health care, is demanding that we become more flexible, more willing to work with other professions collaboratively, and more able to arrive at solutions in nontraditional ways. With shrinking resources, we must be creative, diverse, and, very importantly, proactive in shaping the future of the athletic training profession. Teamwork and knowing how to be a team member are hallmarks of successful professionals and are necessary skills to learn in order to survive, grow, and make a difference in the 21st century.

References

1. McBride J. Job search strategies to begin the next millennium. In: *Planning Job Choices: 1999.* Bethlehem, PA: National Association of Colleges and Employers; 1998.

2. National Athletic Trainers' Association. *Athletic Training Educational Competencies.* Dallas, TX: National Athletic Trainers' Association; 1999.

3. Cherry B, Jacob S. *Contemporary Nursing Issues, Trends, and Management.* St. Louis, MO: Mosby; 1999.

4. Lefton R, Buzzotta V, Sherberg M. *Improving Productivity Through People Skills.* St. Louis, MO: Psychological Associates; 1980.

5. Chance JA. *Continuous Improvement Team Leader and Facilitator Workshop.* West Chester, PA: Newlin Quality Partners; 1997.

Chapter Ten

The Role of Continuous Quality Improvement

"The greatest thing in this world is not so much where we are, but in which direction we are moving."
Oliver Wendell Holmes

OBJECTIVES

On completion of this chapter, the student will be able to accomplish the following:

- Explain continuous quality improvement (CQI) and interpret its five fundamental principles
- Restate the purposes of acquiring continuing education units (CEU) after certification
- Develop a personal rationale for the importance of lifelong learning
- Explain the paradox "we are inundated by information yet starved for knowledge"

This chapter has relevance to the following affective competency from Professional Development and Responsibilities of the *Athletic Training Educational Competencies*[1] (see Appendix A):

- Accepts the professional responsibility to satisfy certified athletic trainers' continuing education requirements

and the following affective competency from Health Care Administration:

- Appreciates the roles and relationship among NATA, NATABOC/NOCA, NCCA, and JRC-AT/CAAHEP

CONTINUOUS QUALITY IMPROVEMENT

CQI is one of several terms (eg, total quality management [TQM], continuous improvement [CI]) borrowed from the business world and used extensively in health care settings, higher education, and government organizations. CQI is a philosophy and a set of guiding principles and practices applied within an organization's strategic management system for improving the quality of any service.[2] Because CQI will be operating in many of the settings where the athletic trainer will be employed, it is important to have a basic understanding of what it is and how it affects every professional entering the organization.

CQI has five fundamental principles:

1. Focused on the mission and vision of the organization
2. Client-centered
3. Data-based
4. Based on consensus decision-making
5. Ongoing (continuous)

Every organization has a vision and/or mission statement. Many departments have their own mission statement that is unique to their expertise, but still relates to the overall vision and mission of the organization. Some businesses, eg, Marriott Hotels, have each employee create his or her own mission statement. A vision is a realistic, credible, attractive future for the organization.[3] For example, when Toyota realized its dream of producing the Lexus, the company's vision was "To produce a vehicle engineered to go beyond existing standards of high-performance luxury automobiles." Vision gives a workplace direction.

A mission statement states the organization's (or employee's) purpose. The purpose of athletic trainers in a university setting has always been, among other things, to provide prevention, care, and rehabilitation of injuries to athletes. However, a particular university's athletic training department may have a vision to be a leader in conducting and publishing research on the effects of open versus closed kinetic chain exercise; an industrial setting may dream about developing a prevention program dedicated to meeting the needs of all employees and reducing time lost from work by 70%. As early as the interview phase of interest in a job, one should know the organization's vision and mission.

The second fundamental is that the organization must be client-centered. The client is seen as anyone who uses or is affected by the service. The organization (or a department) must find out what clients' needs are and then design a service that will meet those needs. Even in education settings, where the athletic training room may have been operating successfully for years, there is always room for determining if the athletes, coaches, and other clients are having their needs met.

The third CQI fundamental is that all decisions must be based on facts/data versus personal opinion or anecdotal information. It is alarming to think that we make decisions based on anything other than facts, but in reality, decisions are made daily that have no facts to support them, just someone's hunch or support of an old policy, no matter what the evidence may now reveal.

The fourth fundamental is ensuring that all major decisions are made using consensus. This means that teams of people make the major decision and that they all must agree to the solution. Often, when a major decision has to be made, committees or departments will discuss the issue and then vote. The people who vote against the majority are left feeling that their ideas were not heard. In consensus decision-making, a discussion occurs and then each person is asked his or her opinion. Once the most popular solution is evident, the chairperson/facilitator asks each individual if he or she can live with that solution for the good of the group. This makes everyone a participant with a vested interest in the solution. Note that consensus is not a unanimous vote—consensus may not represent everyone's first priority. Consensus was discussed in greater detail in Chapter 9. The advantages of team decisions include better ideas, a wider view of the problem, faster implementation of solutions (because all members are in agreement), and a commitment to solutions.

The fifth fundamental is that CQI is continuous. As better ways to do things are identified, the new ways are incorporated, and the CQI fundamentals and processes are continued.

CQI based on the aforementioned fundamentals can be visualized using the Plan—Do—Check—Act cycle (Figure 10-1):

- *Plan* to accomplish the goal. This could be, for example, a new record-keeping plan or a substance abuse prevention plan.
- *Do* the improvement on a small scale (e.g., once you have collected data about the medical record system you will choose, try it with a sampling of your athletics first; or, once you have gathered and analyzed data on which substances your specific teams are most likely to be susceptible to abusing, create a preventative program for just one team).

Figure   10-1.   Plan–Do–Check–Act
Cycle.

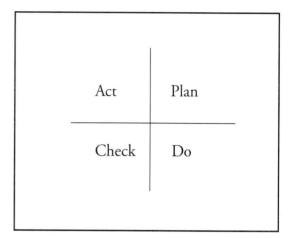

- *Check* the results of your plan by gathering data. Test the results by analyzing the data.
- *Act* on the successful changes by implementing the plan on a larger scale. Make changes to the plan in those areas where expectations were not met. This will ensure that you are continuously improving in that area.

SELF-ASSESSMENT

Whether it is required or not (and it probably will not be), it is a good idea to try to articulate your own individual mission statement. What are you going to do to make yourself successful in your workplace? What is your purpose? Your own values should be reflected in your mission. Periodically, you can pull this statement out and check yourself to see if you are staying true to your purpose. On occasion, you may want to revise the statement. The same CQI principles used in the prior section can be modified to help you achieve personal professional goals.

There are formal self-assessment tools available in almost any area you want to work on for improvement. Instruments (tests) to measure stress levels, assertiveness, time management, self-awareness, values, and many others are available, often through counseling or human resource offices.

CONTINUING EDUCATION

CEU are required of most certified or licensed health care professionals. Professionals are expected to accumulate a minimal number of CEU within a set time frame in order to maintain certification/license. CEU are based on contact hours spent attending or participating in an educational program approved for CEU by the professional organization. The National Athletic Trainers' Association Board of Certification (NATABOC) requires athletic trainers to accumulate CEU every 3 years, including cardiopulmonary resuscitation (CPR) recertification. CPR certification must be current at the time one submits CEU.

> "The purpose of continuing education for the ATC (Athletic Trainer, Certified) is to promote continued competence and development of current knowledge and skills and to enhance professional skills and judgement beyond the levels required for entry-level practice. These activities are deemed necessary to protect the public. Continuing education activities must be directed toward professionals in the athletic training field and must focus on increasing knowledge, skills, and abilities in the practice of athletic training." [4]

The NATA CEU approved provider list is extensive and continues to grow. Each newly certified member is sent a CEU folder packet with an updated provider directory. In order to meet the 3-year CEU requirement, certified athletic trainers can accumulate hours in different categories. He or she may choose CEU from any of the categories but there is a maximum permissible within each category. Acceptable activities include attending symposia, seminars, workshops, and conferences; speaking; authoring; and related activities (such as taking approved home study courses or purchasing and viewing athletic training–related videos) postcertification education at a college or university. Because the CEU requirements are reviewed periodically, every athletic trainer or student should visit the NATABOC website to obtain the most recent information and changes (www.nataboc.org). Maintaining appropriate CEU is one component of the concept referred to as lifelong learning.

LIFELONG LEARNING

In an era of rapidly changing health care, combined with access to increasingly diverse information, it is imperative that professionals make a commitment to lifelong learning. This is often called professional development. We can access information instantaneously from all over the world and new graduates cannot be expected to know all there is to know after their undergraduate and graduate professional preparation. The information explosion, due primarily to sophisticated information highways, has made it impossible to stay current in every aspect of the field.

However, it is necessary to seek out opportunities to learn as much as possible about advances in athletic training and new techniques being developed and used. CEU are a minimal way to accomplish this. There are also other important areas for growth that are indirectly linked to athletic training. For example, keeping abreast of the movements and trends in health care, attending self-improvement seminars (in such fields as leadership, stress management, and team building), becoming knowledgeable about and a participant in strategic planning for one's institution, and attending grant writing workshops will all help the athletic trainer grow professionally.

Peter Drucker, world-renowned management consultant, speaker, and author, says: "We have moved into an economic order in which knowledge, not labor or raw material or capital, is the key resource, a social order in which inequality based on knowledge is a major challenge . . . "[5]

Staying on top of this information explosion will indeed be a challenge. Professional development is not just academic, it is also clinical. Professional development opportunities exist in your daily job; for example, cotreating an athlete with another athletic trainer or physical therapist, or creating a study group or professional journal club, or arranging for a colleague with special expertise to conduct an inservice. Taking courses (credit or noncredit) will also help you to continue your growth.

Employees must be prepared to engage in continuous learning for a lifetime that will probably encompass several different careers. This is the "Knowledge Age" and the launching of an era where one never really finishes with formal instruction and learning.

Dr. William Brody, President of The John Hopkins University, contrasts the Information Age with the Knowledge Age. He describes the Information Age as one of a burden rather than a resource, where most people suffer from information overload (information constantly flowing from newspapers, telephone, fax, e-mail, and Internet).[6] "In fact, what we crave is better access to knowledge, not information. Knowledge is content that is assimilated, collated, and interpreted to provide a unique perspective that helps us perform a task, solve a problem, or stimulate our intellect. The paradox of our times is that we are inundated by information yet starved for knowledge."[6]

Clearly, lifelong learning has become a necessity due to medical advances, new tools/equipment, new training, and an increasingly diverse workforce. Updated training to sharpen thought processes, improve communication skills, multiskill, and keep up with new lifestyles will keep one marketable. With the population aging and many new workers with minimal experience, it is likely that the retirement age will eventually increase to over age 70. Seniors' experiences and skills will need to be shared with younger workers. If one works until age 70, it is obvious that continuous updating of skills and knowledge will be necessary. Investing in lifelong learning will keep us from depreciating.[7]

SUMMARY

CQI, or continuous quality improvement, is a term used in business, health care, and education, and usually relates to processes within the organization. However, it is also relevant to individual and collective professional growth. Knowledge of the employer's mission as well as one's own professional mission helps the employee know if he or she is being successful. Continuing education and lifelong learning opportunities continue to be available. It is necessary to tap into these resources, not only for maintaining CEU for certification, but also for success in a rapidly changing workplace and health care system.

REFERENCES

1. National Athletic Trainers' Association. *Athletic Training Educational Competencies.* Dallas, TX: National Athletic Trainers' Association; 1999.

2. Chance J. *Slippery Rock University Introduction to Continuous Improvement.* Kennett Square, PA: Newlin Quality Partners; 1997.

3. Nanus G. *Visionary Leadership.* San Francisco, CA: Jossey-Bass; 1992.

4. National Athletic Trainers' Association Board of Certification. *2000–2002 Continuing Education Guidelines.* Dallas, TX: NATABOC.

5. Drucker PF. The age of social transformation. *Atlantic Monthly.* 1994;274:53–80.

6. Brody WR. The university in the twenty-first century: adapting to stay relevant. *Continuing Higher Education Review.* 1988;62:28–39.

7. Eurich NP. *The Learning Industry: Education for Adult Workers.* Princeton, NJ: The Carnegie Foundation for the Advancement of Teaching; 1990.

 *Appendix A*

SELECT NATIONAL ATHLETIC TRAINERS' ASSOCIATION AFFECTIVE COMPETENCIES

Affective Domain (Health Care Administration)

1. Appreciates the roles and responsibilities of medical and allied health care providers, and respects the systems that each provider works within.

2. Appreciates the roles and functions of various medical and paramedical specialties as well as their respective areas of expertise in the acute care of injuries and illnesses to athletes and others involved in physical activity.

3. Values the need for sideline emergency care supplies and equipment as deemed necessary for all athletic training settings.

4. Appreciates the importance of an emergency action plan that is tailored for a specific venue or setting.

5. Accepts the value of a common medical language and terminology to communicate within and between the health professions.

6. Accepts the professional, ethical, and legal parameters that define the proper role of the certified athletic trainer in the administration and implementation of health care delivery systems.

7. Appreciates the roles and relationship between the NATA, NATABOC/NOCA, NCCA, and JRC-AT/CAAHEP.

8. Recognizes and accepts the need for organizing and conducting health care programs for athletes and other physically active individuals on the basis of sound administrative policies and procedures.

9. Accepts the responsibility for completing the necessary paperwork and maintaining the records associated with the administration of health care programs.

10. Respects the roles and cooperation of medical personnel, administrators, and other staff members in the organization and administration of athletic training service programs.

11. Recognizes and accepts the importance of good public relations with the media (radio, TV, press), the general public, other medical and allied health care personnel, and legislators.

12. Recognizes the certified athletic trainer's role as a liaison between athletes, physically active individuals, caretakers, employers, physicians, coaches, other health care professionals, and any individual who may be involved with the care provided by the certified athletic trainer.

Affective Domain (Professional Development and Responsibilities)

1. Accepts the professional responsibility to satisfy certified athletic trainers' continuing education requirements.

2. Appreciates the need for and the process and benefits of athletic training regulatory acts (registration, licensure, certification).

3. Realizes that the state regulatory acts regarding the practice of athletic training vary from state to state.

4. Understands the consequences of noncompliance with regulatory athletic training practice acts.

5. Accepts the professional, historical, ethical, and organizational structures that define the proper roles and responsibilities of the certified athletic trainer in providing health care to athletes and others involved in physical activity.

6. Defends the moral and ethical responsibility to intervene in situations that conflict with NATA standards.

7. Accepts the function of professional organization position statements that relate to athletic training practice.

8. Advocates the NATA as an allied health professional organization for the care of athletes and others involved in physical activity.

9. Respects the role and responsibilities of the other health care professions.

10. Appreciates the dynamic nature of issues and concerns as they relate to the health care of athletes and others involved in physical activity.

11. Defends the responsibility to interpret and promote athletic training as a professional discipline among allied health professional groups and the general public.

12. Accepts the responsibility to enhance the professional growth of athletic training students, colleagues, and peers through a continual sharing of knowledge skills, values, and professional recognition.

From the National Athletic Trainers' Association. Athletic Training Educational Competencies. *Dallas, TX: National Athletic Trainers' Association; 1999. Reprinted with permission of the National Athletic Trainers' Association. Dallas, TX. All rights reserved.*

Appendix B

NATIONAL ATHLETIC TRAINERS' ASSOCIATION EDUCATION TASK FORCE RECOMMENDATIONS

Provision 1: The NATA should work with the NATABOC to institute a requirement, to take effect in 2004, that in order to be eligible for NATABOC certification, all candidates must possess a baccalaureate degree and have successfully completed a CAAHEP accredited entry-level athletic training education program.

Provision 2: The NATA should encourage the development of accredited entry-level post-baccalaureate certificate programs in athletic training and allow these programs to consider an applicant's previous didactic and clinical experience as a partial criterion for admission. The NATA should encourage the development of 2-3, 3-2, 4-1, and other creative models for entry-level education.

Provision 3: The NATA should develop and implement a program leading to certificates of advanced qualification (CAQ) for athletic trainer educators. The educational content of these continuing education courses would be developed by the NATA Education Council (see Provision 8). Certification of competence of the participants and the subsequent awarding of the credential should be contracted to the NATABOC.

Provision 4: The NATA should recommend to the JRC-AT that the CAAHEP Essentials & Guidelines, section II.B.2.b., be modified to reflect formal instruction in pharmacology and pathology.

Provision 5: The NATA should recommend that the NATABOC reevaluate the minimum number of hours necessary to sit for the certification examination and that the present high-risk sport requirement be reevaluated.

Provision 6: The NATA should recommend that the JRC-AT investigate the extent to which the various practice settings in which athletic trainers are commonly employed are incorporated into the clinical and didactic components of the education programs.

Provision 7: The NATA should subcontract the accreditation of accredited master's degree programs in athletic training to the JRC-AT.

Provision 8: The NATA should reconfigure the way professional education is organized. The NATA should establish an Education Council to act as the clearinghouse for educational policy, development, and delivery in our profession. Specific functions of the Education Council should include, but not be limited to, the following:

- Maintain a constant dialogue on accreditation of entry-level programs through its association with the JRC-AT.
- Maintain a constant dialogue on accreditation of master's degree programs through its association with the JRC-AT.
- Act as a resource for the development of doctoral programs in athletic training.
- Coordinate the educational content and delivery of all NATA-sponsored continuing education and CAQ programs.
- Serve as a resource to district, state, and local continuing education program planners.
- Act as the approval agency for certifying continuing education providers.
- Develop new technologies for the delivery of continuing education programs.

The Education Council should replace the present Professional Education Committee. This provision is contingent upon approval of Provision 7.

Provision 9: The NATA should cooperate with the NATABOC in its ongoing evaluation of the new rules for CEU accumulation and recertification.

Provision 10: The NATA should develop and implement a program leading to certificates of advanced qualification (CAQ) for the post-entry level athletic trainer. The educational content of these continuing education courses would be developed by the NATA Education Council (see Provision 8). Certification of competence of the participants and the subsequent awarding of the credential should be contracted to the NATABOC. By the year 2000 an inaugural CAQ program should be made available.

Provision 11: The NATA should encourage the development of multi-disciplinary education programs that coordinate athletic training with teaching, nursing, physical therapy, occupational therapy, or other appropriate baccalaureate level professions.

Provision 12: The NATA should encourage new athletic training education programs to consider aligning themselves in colleges of health-related professions.

Provision 13: The NATA should strongly encourage athletic training education programs to title their programs as "Athletic Training."

Provision 14: The NATA should encourage the Research and Education Foundation, the *Journal of Athletic Training*, and other appropriate entities to continue to recognize and reward high quality research in those areas of the body of knowledge specific to athletic training.

Provision 15: The NATA should encourage and assist in initiating the process of legislative reform, with particular emphasis on standardization of educational requirements for state credentialing.

Provision 16: The NATA should work to identify and promote positive work models for the high school environment including, but not limited to, the full-time athletic trainer and the teacher–athletic trainer.

Provision 17: The NATA should encourage and provide assistance to the JRC-AT for the process of helping them contract their administrative functions with a professional management firm.

Provision 18: The NATA should collaborate with the NATAREF to make planning grants available to those institutions that wish to make the transition from the internship to the accredited model, but whose financial or historical situation hinders them from doing so.

Recommendations to reform athletic training education. NATA News, *1997; Feb:16–24. Reprinted with permission from the National Athletic Trainers' Association.*

Appendix C

NATIONAL ATHLETIC TRAINERS'
ASSOCIATION CODE OF ETHICS

Preamble

The Code of Ethics of the National Athletic Trainers' Association has been written to make the membership aware of the principles of ethical behavior that should be followed in the practice of athletic training. The primary goal of the Code is the assurance of high quality health care. The Code presents aspirational standards of behavior that all members should strive to achieve.

The principles cannot be expected to cover all specific situations that may be encountered by the practicing athletic trainer, but should be considered representative of the spirit with which athletic trainers make decisions. The principles are written generally and the circumstances of a situation will determine the interpretation and application of a given principle and of the Code as a whole. Whenever there is a conflict between the Code and legality, the laws prevail. The guidelines set forth in this Code are subject to continual review and revision as the athletic training profession develops and changes.

Principle 1: Members shall respect the rights, welfare, and dignity of all individuals.

1.1 Members shall not discriminate against any legally protected class.

1.2 Members shall be committed to providing competent care consistent with both the requirements and the limitations of their profession.

1.3 Members shall preserve the confidentiality of privileged information and shall not release such information to a third party not involved in the patient's care unless the person consents to such release or release is permitted or required by law.

Principle 2: Members shall comply with the laws and regulations governing the practice of athletic training.

2.1 Members shall comply with applicable local, state, and federal laws and institutional guidelines.

2.2 Members shall be familiar with and adhere to all National Athletic Trainers' Association guidelines and ethical standards.

2.3 Members are encouraged to report illegal or unethical practice pertaining to athletic training to the appropriate person or authority.

2.4 Members shall avoid substance abuse and, when necessary, seek rehabilitation for chemical dependency.

Principle 3: Members shall accept responsibility for the exercise of sound judgment.

3.1 Members shall not misrepresent in any manner, either directly or indirectly, their skills, training, professional credentials, identity, or services.

3.2 Members shall provide only those services for which they are qualified via education and/or experience and by pertinent legal regulatory process.

3.3 Members shall provide services, make referrals, and seek compensation only for those services that are necessary.

Principle 4: Members shall maintain and promote high standards in the provision of services.

4.1 Members shall recognize the need for continuing education and participate in various types of educational activities that enhance their skills and knowledge.

4.2 Members who have the responsibility for employing and evaluating the performance of other staff members shall fulfill such responsibility in a fair, considerate, and equitable manner, on the basis of clearly enunciated criteria.

4.3 Members who have the responsibility for evaluating the performance of employees, supervisees, or students are encouraged to share evaluations with them and allow them the opportunity to respond to those evaluations.

4.4 Members shall educate those whom they supervise in the practice of athletic training with regard to the Code of Ethics and encourage their adherence to it.

4.5 Whenever possible, members are encouraged to participate and support others in the conduct and communication of research and educational activities that may contribute knowledge for improved patient care, patient or student education, and the growth of athletic training as a profession.

4.6 When members are researchers or educators, they are responsible for maintaining and promoting ethical conduct in research and educational activities.

Principle 5: Members shall not engage in any form of conduct that constitutes a conflict of interest or that adversely reflects on the profession.

5.1 The private conduct of the member is a personal matter to the same degree as is any other person's except when such conduct compromises the fulfillment of professional responsibilities.

5.2 Members of the National Athletic Trainers' Association and others serving on the Association's committees or acting as consultants shall not use, directly or by implication, the Association's name or logo or their affiliation with the Association in the endorsement of products or services.

5.3 Members shall not place financial gain above the welfare of the patient being treated and shall not participate in any arrangement that exploits the patient.

5.4 Members may seek remuneration for their services that is commensurate with their services and in compliance with applicable law.

National Athletic Trainers' Association, 1997. Reprinted with permission of the National Athletic Trainers' Association.

 Appendix D

CODE OF ETHICS OF THE
AMERICAN PHYSICAL THERAPY ASSOCIATION

Preamble

This Code of Ethics sets forth ethical principles for the physical therapy profession. Members of this profession are responsible for maintaining and promoting ethical practice. This Code of Ethics, adopted by the American Physical Therapy Association, shall be binding on physical therapists who are members of the Association.

Principle 1: Physical therapists respect the rights and dignity of all individuals.

Principle 2: Physical therapists comply with the laws and regulations governing the practice of physical therapy.

Principle 3: Physical therapists accept responsibility for the exercise of sound judgment.

Principle 4: Physical therapists maintain and promote high standards for physical therapy practice, education, and research.

Principle 5: Physical therapists seek remuneration for their services that is deserved and reasonable.

Principle 6: Physical therapists provide accurate information to the consumer about the profession and about those services they provide.

Principle 7: Physical therapists accept the responsibility to protect the public and the profession from unethical, incompetent, or illegal acts.

Principle 8: Physical therapists participate in efforts to address the health needs of the public.

Adopted by APTA House of Delegates, June 1981. Amended June 1987 and June 1991. Reprinted with permission of the American Physical Therapy Association.

Appendix E

NATIONAL ATHLETIC TRAINERS' ASSOCIATION
MEMBERSHIP SANCTIONS AND PROCEDURES

Grounds for Sanctions

When a person becomes a member of NATA, he or she assumes certain obligations and responsibilities. A member is responsible for dues as provided and specified by the by-laws or other governing provisions. A member may be subject to one or more of the sanctions set forth in Section III G, below, if his or her conduct falls within one of the following categories:

1. Misstatement of a material fact or failure to state a material fact in an application for membership, or in any other manner obtaining or attempting to obtain NATA membership by fraud or deception;

2. Knowingly assisting another to obtain or attempt to obtain NATA membership by false statement, fraud, or deception;

3. Misrepresentation of NATA membership status;

4. Misrepresentation of NATA certification status, or other professional qualification or credentials;

5. The conviction of, plea of guilty, or plea of *nolo contendere* to a felony which is directly related to public health or athletic care or education. This includes but is not limited to a felony involving: rape; sexual abuse of an athlete or child; actual or threatened use of a weapon or violence; the prohibited sale or distribution of a controlled substance, or its possession with the intent to distribute; or use of position of athletic trainer improperly (i) to influence or attempt to influence the outcome or score of an athletic event or (ii) in connection with any gambling activity.

6. Serious or repeated violations of the NATA's Charter, By-laws, Code of Ethics, policies, rules, or standards.

Panels

1. With general oversight from the NATA Board of Directors, the NATA Ethics Committee, by majority vote, shall select persons who are NATA members to form (i) an Investigative Panel of NATA members, (ii) a Fact-Finding Panel of NATA members, and (iii) an Appellate Panel of NATA members, to address alleged violations of the standards set forth in Sections III A(1)–(6), above. The majority of each of these panels shall consist of Ethics Committee members, and a majority of each of the Presiding Panels selected to handle individual cases shall, if possible, be Ethics Committee members. The Ethics Committee shall attempt to staff Presiding Panels with members from (a) a variety of practice settings, (b) geographically diverse locations, and (c) diverse backgrounds and levels of experience.

2. The terms of the members of each of the three Panels shall run for 2 years and may be renewed.

3. A majority of the members of each Panel shall annually elect the Chair of the Panel.

4. In every individual case, three members of the Investigative Panel shall carry out the requisite investigative function; three members of the Fact-Finding Panel shall carry out the requisite hearing function; and three members of the Appellate Panel (one Ethics Committee member, one at-large member, and one director from the Board) shall carry out the requisite appellate function. The Chair of each Panel shall determine the identify of the Presiding Panel members assigned to carry out such functions in each case, after due consideration is given to fairness, efficiency, and convenience to all concerned.

5. In every individual case, NATA shall, upon written request from the Investigative or Fact-Finding Panels, provide to said Panels all information in the custody of NATA related to the NATA applicant or member in question. Each NATA applicant or member in question shall release, discharge, and exonerate NATA, its officers, directors, employees, committee members, and agents furnishing said information, from any and all liability of any nature and kind arising out of or relating to the furnishing of said information.

6. No NATA member shall serve concurrently on more than one of the three Panels.

7. No NATA member shall serve on more than one Presiding Panel in the same case.

8. No member of any of the three Panels shall participate in any case where his or her impartiality or the presence of an actual, potential, or apparent conflict of interest might reasonably be questioned.

9. When a vacancy occurs on one of the three Panels, the Ethics Committee by majority vote shall promptly elect a replacement from among the NATA membership.

Reporting of Violations

NATA members who have information with regard to allegations raising issues under Sections III A (1)–(6), above, and wishing to supply such information to NATA, shall supply this information, with as much specificity and documentation as possible, to NATA's Executive Director or Chair of the Ethics Committee. If a NATA member supplies information to only one of these two individuals, the individual receiving the information shall notify the other, and supply copies of any letters or other documents received. If a NATA member, or someone who is not a NATA member, supplies information concerning a possible violation of NATA standards to a NATA member other than the Executive Director or the Ethics Committee Chair, that member may forward the information to the Executive Director or Ethics Committee Chair, or encourage the individual or individuals supplying the information to do so.

Information need not be supplied in writing, and the reporting NATA member need not identify him- or herself. However, NATA's Executive Director and Ethics Committee Chair will not forward information that is too vague, information that cannot be substantiated without the assistance of the reporting person, or information where, in the opinion of the NATA Executive Director and Ethics Chair, there is no need for anonymity for the reporting individual. A member may report information on the condition that the member's name or certain other facts be kept confidential. NATA may proceed with an investigation subject to such a condition; however, NATA must inform the reporting member that at some point in the investigation NATA may determine that it cannot proceed further without disclosing some of the confidential information, either to the applicant or member under investigation or to some other party. A reporting member, upon receiving this information from NATA, may decide whether or not to allow the information to be revealed. If the reporting member decides that the necessary information must remain confidential, NATA may be required to close the unfinished investigation for lack of necessary information. NATA members are strongly encouraged to provide information, with as much detail as possible, in writing.

Investigation

1. Whenever the Chair of the Investigative Panel receives allegations which in his or her judgment sufficiently and meaningfully raise the possibility of violations of Sections III A (1)–(6), above, by a NATA applicant or member, the Investigative Panel, through a Presiding Panel composed of three (3) members appointed by the Chair, shall conduct a preliminary inquiry into the matter. Upon commencing such a preliminary inquiry, the Chair of the Investigative Panel shall by certified mail, return receipt requested, notify the NATA applicant or member in question that such an inquiry is being conducted and shall state the provisions of the Membership Standards relating to said preliminary inquiry. This notification shall be provided in or consistent with the form specified by NATA's counsel, and shall be reviewed by NATA's Executive Director or counsel prior to mailing.

2. If the three-member Presiding Investigative Panel by majority vote determines that there is good cause to believe that a more formal and thorough investigation need be conducted, such an investigation shall commence. If such an investigation commences, the Chair of the Presiding Investigative Panel shall by certified mail, return receipt requested, so notify the NATA applicant or member in question and shall specify the provisions of the Membership Standards relating to said formal investigation.

3. If the three-member Presiding Investigative Panel by majority vote determines that no good cause exists to question compliance with the relevant Membership Standards, no further action shall be taken. The inquiry shall be closed, and the Chair of the Presiding Investigative Panel shall, by certified mail, return receipt requested, so notify the NATA applicant or member in question, the Chair of NATA's Ethics Committee, and NATA's Executive Director.

4. If, after formal investigation, the three-member Presiding Investigative Panel by majority vote determines that there is good cause to believe that the NATA applicant or member in question has violated one or more of the Membership Standards, the Chair of the Presiding Investigative Panel shall, after appropri-

ate review by counsel, forward to said NATA applicant or member by certified mail, return receipt requested, a detailed statement ("Statement of Allegations") setting forth:

(a) The Membership Standards allegedly violated;

(b) A summary of the Presiding Investigative Panel's allegations and charges;

(c) A summary of the evidence establishing the alleged violation of the Membership Standards;

(d) The possible sanctions for the alleged violations;

(e) Notification that the NATA applicant or member in question has the right to legal counsel in all subsequent proceedings;

(f) Notification that the NATA applicant or member in question has the right to request an oral and/or written hearing before the NATA Fact-Finding Panel with respect to the Statement of Allegations, with said applicant or member bearing his or her own expenses for such hearings;

(g) Notification that the NATA applicant or member in question shall have twenty-one (21) days after receipt of the Statement Allegations:

to notify the Panel if he or she disputes the allegations or possible sanctions set forth in the Statement of Allegations;

to submit a brief written response setting forth the applicant's or member's reasons for disputing the Statement of Allegations; and

to request an oral and/or written hearing;

(h) Notification that the NATA applicant or member in question, in any matter in which a possible sanction is one of those listed in Sections III G 2 (a)–(e) below, may appear in person before the Presiding Fact-Finding Panel with the assistance of counsel, may make opening statements, present documents and testimony, examine and cross-examine witnesses under oath, make closing statements, and present written submissions on his or her behalf;

(i) Notification that the NATA applicant or member in question, in any matter in which the possible sanctions are only those listed in Sections III G 2 (f)–(i) below, may request an oral hearing by telephone conference call with the Presiding Fact-Finding Panel, at which time the NATA applicant or member in question may participate with the assistance of counsel, may make appropriate statements or arguments, and may respond to questions from the Presiding Panel;

(j) Notification that the NATA applicant or member in question may in any matter, if he or she wishes, waive oral hearing and merely submit written materials to the Presiding Fact-Finding Panel in response to the Statement of Allegations, on a schedule to be established by the Fact-Finding Panel;

(k) Notification that the establishment of the truth of the Statement of Allegations or the failure to respond thereto may result in the levying of any or all of the sanctions listed in the Statement of Allegations upon the NATA applicant or member in question;

(l) Notification that if the NATA applicant or member in question does not dispute the Statement of Allegations, he or she consents that the Investigative Panel may refer the matter to the Fact-Finding Panel which may render a decision and levy appropriate sanctions.

5. If the NATA applicant or member in question disputes in any way the allegations or sanctions set forth in the Statement of Allegations, the Chair of the Investigative Panel shall forward the matter and the entire record thereof to the Chair of the Fact-Finding Panel.

6. All decisions of the three member Investigative Panel shall be considered the decisions of the entire Investigative Panel.

Fact Finding

1. After receipt of the record of a matter from the Chair of the Investigative Panel, the Chair of the Fact-Finding Panel shall with reasonable expedition:

   (a) appoint three members of the Panel, two of whom are Ethics Committee members, to preside over the matter;

   (b) schedule an appropriate hearing before the Presiding Panel members;

   (c) forward to the NATA applicant or member in question by certified mail, return receipt requested, a Notice of Hearing setting forth the identity of the Presiding Panel members and the date of the hearing.

2. The Fact-Finding Presiding Panel shall tape record all oral hearings.

3. In any matter in which a hearing is requested and a possible sanction is one of those listed in Sections III G 2 (a)–(e) below, the NATA and the applicant or member in question may make opening statements, present documents and testimony, examine and cross-examine witnesses under oath, make closing statements, and tender written submissions as permitted and scheduled by the Presiding Panel member. In all other matters in which a hearing is requested, both NATA and the applicant or member in question shall submit their contentions in writing as and when directed by the Presiding Panel members.

4. The Presiding Panel members shall determine all matters relating to the hearing. All decisions of the Presiding Panel shall be considered the decision of the entire Fact-Finding Panel.

5. If the Presiding Panel members, after a full and fair hearing, determine that the preponderance of the evidence does not establish any violation of the Membership Standards, no further action shall be taken. The case shall be closed, and the Presiding Panel shall, by certified mail, return receipt requested, so notify the NATA applicant or member in question, the Chair of NATA's Ethics Committee, and NATA's Executive Director.

6. If the Presiding Panel members, after a full and fair hearing, determine that the preponderance of the evidence does establish that a provision of the Membership Standards has been violated, the Chair of the Presiding Panel shall prepare a written decision setting forth:

    (a) the Membership Standards that have been violated;

    (b) findings of fact establishing said violations;

    (c) appropriate sanctions; and

    (d) other relevant and appropriate information.

7. The Chair of the Fact-Finding Panel shall promptly forward a copy of the Presiding Panel's decision to the NATA applicant or member in question by certified mail, return receipt requested. The Chair shall also notify the NATA applicant or member in question in writing that he or she has the right to appeal the decision by submitting to the Chair of the Fact-Finding Panel a Notice of Appeal within ten (10) days of his or her receipt of the decision.

8. Upon receipt of a Notice of Appeal in any case, the Chair of the Fact-Finding Panel shall forward said Notice and the rest of the record of the case to the Chair of the Appellate Panel.

9. In every case in which the NATA applicant or member in question chooses not to appeal the decision of the presiding member of the Fact-Finding Presiding Panel, that decision shall be the final decision in the matter.

10. When a decision of the Presiding Fact-Finding Panel is final, and the NATA applicant or member chooses not to appeal the decision, the Chair of the Fact-Finding Panel shall notify the Chair of the Investigative Panel, the Chair of the Ethics Committee, and NATA's Executive Director that a final decision has been reached, and shall notify each as to the nature of the decision. The Chair of the Fact-Finding Panel shall then turn over the complete file of the case to NATA's Executive Director.

Evidence

Formal rules of evidence shall not apply in any hearing before Fact-Finding Presiding Panels. Relevant evidence shall be admitted in all hearings. The Presiding Panel member shall resolve all questions disputed at the hearing, and notify counsel of its decisions with appropriate opportunity for review, before any sanctions are levied.

Sanctions

1. Sanctions for violations of any Membership Standard shall in all cases be reasonable in all the circumstances.

2. Such sanctions may include one or more of the following:

    (a) denial of eligibility;

    (b) cancellation of membership;

    (c) non-renewal of membership;

    (d) suspension of membership;

    (e) public censure;

    (f) private reprimand;

    (g) required training or other corrective action;

    (h) written reports with limited circulation; and

    (i) conditions related to the above.

Appeal

1. Upon receipt of a Notice of Appeal and the remaining record of a case from the Chair of the Fact-Finding Panel, the Chair of the Appellate Panel shall:

(a) appoint three members of the Appellate Panel (one Ethics Committee member, one at-large member, and one director from the Board) to preside over the appeal;

(b) set a briefing schedule pursuant to which both NATA and the appealing NATA applicant or member may present their contentions in writing to the Presiding Panel with respect to the decision of the Fact-Finding Panel. For purposes of this presentation, NATA shall be represented by a member of the Ethics Committee, selected by the Committee, who is not or was not sitting on any panel involved with the case being appealed, and the written submission of that representative shall have been reviewed by NATA's Executive Director and approved by NATA's counsel; and

(c) set a date for oral hearing either in person or by telephone conference call at the option of NATA, taking into account the seriousness of the allegations and the wishes of the NATA applicant or member. At the hearing, both NATA and the appealing NATA applicant or member may participate with counsel before the Presiding Panel;

(d) formal rules of evidence shall not apply in any hearing before the Presiding Appellate Panel. Relevant evidence shall be admitted in all hearings. The Presiding Panel members shall resolve all questions disputed at the hearing, and shall notify counsel of its decisions with appropriate opportunity for review, before any sanctions are levied.

2. After oral hearing and due consideration, the Presiding Panel shall render a decision in writing affirming, reversing, or modifying the decision of the Fact-Finding Panel. The decision of the Presiding Panel shall be considered the decision of the entire Appellate Panel. The decision of the presiding Panel members shall set forth the Panel's factual findings as well as the rationale for decision with respect to any violations of the Membership Standards and the levying of sanctions.

3. In every case in which a NATA applicant or member exercises his or her appellate rights, the decision of the Appellate Panel shall be the final decision in the matter.

National Athletic Trainers' Association Code of Ethics, 1997. Reprinted with permission of the National Athletic Trainers' Association.

Index

BUILD *Your Library*

This book and many others on numerous different topics are available from SLACK Incorporated. For further information or a copy of our latest catalog, contact us at:

Professional Book Division
SLACK Incorporated
6900 Grove Road
Thorofare, NJ 08086 USA
Telephone: 1-856-848-1000
1-800-257-8290
Fax: 1-856-853-5991
E-mail: orders@slackinc.com
www.slackbooks.com

We accept most major credit cards and checks or money orders in US dollars drawn on a US bank. Most orders are shipped within 72 hours.

Contact us for information on recent releases, forthcoming titles, and bestsellers. If you have a comment about this title or see a need for a new book, direct your correspondence to the Editorial Director at the above address.

Thank you for your interest and we hope you found this work beneficial.